OUT OF THE FOG, INTO THE CLEAR;

Journaling to Help You Heal from Toxic Relationships

Shannon D. Petrovich,
LCSW, LISAC, BCD

Kindle Dirct Publishing

Copyright © 2022 Shannon Petrovich

All rights reserved

No part of this book may be reproduced, or stored in a retrieval system, or transmitted in any form or by any means, electronic, mechanical, photocopying, recording, or otherwise, without express written permission of the publisher.

ISBN-13: 9798830908498
ISBN-10: 1477123456

Cover design by: Shannon Petrovich,
Photography by: William Carson Dexter
Library of Congress Control Number: 2018675309
Printed in the United States of America

Dedication;
To my husband who has been incredibly supportive and is my lighthouse in every storm and fog.
To my Mom and Dad, who raised us to be tenacious, adventurous, and compassionate; a combination which proved problematic at times in my youth, but now has been key to driving this project from conception to completion.
To all those I've seen do this work on yourselves over the years; your courage, strength and wisdom live in these pages.
And to those just beginning your journey out of the fog; you are the inspiration for this book, and I hope and pray it helps guide you gently into safe harbor.

CONTENTS

Title Page
Copyright
Dedication
Introduction
Part 1; The FOG ... 1
Chapter 1; Finding Yourself in the FOG ... 2
Chapter 2; Fear, Obligation, and Guilt ... 8
Chapter 3; Taking Stock of the Abusive Relationship ... 12
Chapter 4; Beliefs, Behaviors, Attitudes, and Attributes of Toxic, Abusive and Narcissistic People. ... 25
Chapter 5; Trauma-Bonding; ... 30
Chapter 6; Placating, People-pleasing, and Peacekeeping; ... 33
Part 2; Getting CLEAR ... 39
Chapter 7; C is for Clarity ... 40
Chapter 8; L is for Leaving; ... 44
Chapter 9; E is for Educate ... 58
Chapter 10; A is for Awareness ... 68
Chapter 11; R is for Rebuilding ... 75
Chapter 12; Stress Strategies ... 95
Chapter 13; Loving Again… or Not?! ... 99
Chapter 14; Habits VS. Motivation ... 102

Chapter 15; Final Thoughts and Journaling 103
About The Author 105

INTRODUCTION

In my 35 years as a therapist, I've worked with thousands of people, and found that much of it has been focused on helping people heal from toxic or abusive relationships. My first therapeutic job was as a volunteer in a domestic violence shelter, where we supported victims, and I ran art therapy support groups for their children. From then until now, whether male or female, small children or elderly, helping others clear their way after having been emotionally, and/or physically beaten down by another has been my life's work. This book is the culmination of that work in the form of a journaling workbook. I chose this format because merely finding insights through reading is not what it takes to heal. Each must navigate their journey through the fog, and this workbook, with its hundreds of journal prompts throughout, is designed to help you do just that.

In June of 2018, after several very high-profile suicides, and an overall escalation of poor mental health across the world, my concern for the thousands, perhaps even millions of people who have no access to mental health help reached a fever pitch. I decided to start TherapistTalks, a YouTube channel to share insights, information, and strategies to help people struggling with various mental health issues. Though my videos are very homespun and rough, they've been viewed over 1.3 million times for over 130,000 view-hours by people from all around the world; clearly there is a serious need! The most viewed videos are about dealing with, setting boundaries around, getting free from, and healing from toxic, narcissistic, and abusive relationships. These have included relationships with a partner, parent, adult child, sibling, co-worker, or friend. If you've sought help with these struggles, this workbook is for you. In these pages you'll find the information, insights, and strategies to walk through these most challenging times.

There is a lot of focus on labels these days, and many people are hung up on armchair diagnosing their abusive partner, parent, sibling, son, daughter or friend as a 'narcissist.' Though the toxic person in your life may or may not have narcissistic traits, or even the full-blown disorder, we are not going to focus on *them*, but on YOU; your self-discovery, your healing, your journey, your new boundaries, and self-care. I'm using the terms 'toxic' or 'abusive,' to focus on the *behaviors* that have harmed you, no matter where they are coming from. This is part of your healing too; to stop ruminating on what is wrong with *them and* start taking care of *you*.

Of course, it's always best to have your own therapist and this book does not come close to replacing the experience of having someone to help you at every step and stage. If you can access a therapist, please do! And if you do, you can still use this book as an add-on to support your healing journey with your therapist. But most people have no access to therapy, and if this is you, my hope is that this book will offer strategies and perspectives to help you on this very challenging journey back to yourself.

Throughout this workbook, you'll find journal prompts. You can use these prompts to write, simply ponder, or to guide you to talk through this journey with your therapist, trusted friend, or family member. I want to encourage you to spend time with each question in a quiet place, where you can allow yourself to feel and think on a deeper level.

I hope this will guide you to put your new insights into practice, launching your life journey onto a brighter and healthier course, finding the freedom and healing you so want and deserve.

Welcome to the work! All the best, Shannon

If you are in immediate crisis, please call or text one of the many national or local helplines.

http://www.crisitextline.org

National Domestic Violence Hotline
Hours: 24/7. Languages: English, Spanish and 200+ through interpretation service
800-799-7233
National Sexual Assault Hotline
Hours: Available 24 hours
1-800-656-4673
National Suicide Prevention Lifeline
Hours: Available 24 hours. Languages: English, Spanish.
800-273-8255

PART 1; THE FOG

CHAPTER 1; FINDING YOURSELF IN THE FOG

I've been a lifelong sailor, and dense fog is one of the most terrifying and mystifying things I've ever experienced. It can settle in so gradually that you are not even aware your vision is being obscured or descend on you so quickly that the sudden complete bleakness is paralyzing. It's just water vapor after all, what could possibly be so serious about that? But when this happens to you out on the ocean; when the reality hits that you are completely immersed in dense fog, the panic is real. You whirl around in all directions trying to find your bearings, looking for anything that will orient you, and literally you can't see anything but fog. The disorientation is overwhelming; you have no idea where you are, what your boat is doing, where the land or other boats may be, and you know that you are at the whim and will of any danger nearby. Your head pounds, your heart races, your thoughts spin, and you frantically try to grab onto something of substance. But there is nothing, in all directions, but this thick, dense water vapor; nothing but fog. You can't move for fear of running into something, and even staying still is not safe. This frozen state doesn't help you get out of the fog, but feels like your only option. So you sit and wait for the fog to lift.

In the fog of a hurtful relationship, this feeling of paralysis, anxiety, depression, confusion, disorientation, not knowing who you are, or how you got to this dark place in your life, is also real. Others may not understand, and may even get frustrated with you for not getting out of the relationship, but in this state, only you know how simple that sounds, and how hard it really is. The Fear, Obligation, and Guilt crept into your relationship so stealthily that you didn't notice it; the games, the pressures, the gaslighting, the bits of anger, the confusion, the disorientation, all of it was just a bit of water vapor that was easily dismissed. But over the months, or years, the fog set in. Abusive relationships are not an act of nature like ocean fog; they are the result of intentional tactics of manipulation, and control. In the early stages it is hard to see this for what it is. Unfortunately, the fog of an abusive relationship is not going to just lift; nothing will change until *you change it*. So how do you find your bearings, push past this paralysis, clear away your vision, begin to heal the trauma, and rebuild your life?

Internal Self-Talk; Are You in an Abusive Relationship with Yourself?

If your home went through a hurricane, you could walk around afterwards and look at what's damaged. But a superficial walk around won't show you how the frame, foundation, and internal systems were affected, so it is crucial to take a deeper look, probably involving experienced tradespeople of all sorts, who will dig into the walls, assess the foundation, get into each and every wall and pull it all apart. In the same way, you often don't know what's been hurt within yourself or how to care for yourself in the midst of this crisis, unless you open up and take a good look into your foundation, systems and framework. Without that thorough look into your home, you can end up with serious problems and dangers in the future. And without taking a deeper assessment into *yourself*, you often continue to use this broken internal framework to put yourself into ongoing danger in your life.

So let's look at this crisis as an opportunity to walk boldly into your internal basement, and with a strong flashlight of support, look honestly at what's there. With this book as that flashlight and the journaling the path through what is stored there, let's take a deep breath and trudge down those creaky stairs.

<u>Journal;</u>
In the midst of this crisis, what are you noticing you're saying to yourself inside your head? Be honest; include the good, the bad, and the most ugly.

For many the answer to this question leads to a shocking truth; you may be berating yourself mercilessly inside your own head. Often this internal self-talk is as harsh as the verbal abuse you heard in your toxic relationship. The truth is, how we talk to ourselves internally is often worse than anyone could ever say or do to us from the outside, and often we are only marginally aware of this. Usually this starts in early childhood, perhaps in later teen years, and the amount of stress it causes is extreme. It is truly crucial to notice this internal self-talk, as you are already under extreme stress coming out of an abusive relationship, but when you add the self-judgment, the self-deprecation, and self-hatred statements, going on 40,000 times a day inside your head, you can really tank your emotions into a deep dark place.

<u>Journal;</u>
Do you have an awareness of who originally hurt you with those hateful thoughts and words? Or, if no one actually said those things to you, can you identify the experiences you had that may have led you to believe there was something wrong with you that was causing the dysfunction in your life? Write about the person, people, or experiences that taught you to feel this way about yourself.

<u>The Reactive Mind and the Rational Mind;</u>

It's important to recognize that we have a reactive part of our mind called the amygdala, which sees danger and stress, and shoots adrenalin into our system to give us the ability to fight, flight, or freeze. We also have our higher cortex which is our rational judgment center. This gives us the ability to work through stresses rationally. While our reactive mind is impulsive and instinctive, our rational mind is logical and steady. Having an understanding of these two parts of our mind is essential to much of what we will do as we work on healing. Ultimately we need to become aware of our initial _reactions_ to incoming experiences, so that with awareness and practice, we can learn to calm the reactivity of the amygdala, with self-calming exercises. When this is accomplished, we can take the incoming experience _upstairs_ into our higher cortex, where we can reason and rationalize through it, and _choose_ how to _respond_. When we get stuck in our reactive amygdala, our responses are isolated to fight, flight or freeze. However, when we are able to utilize our rational mind, we can slow down our reaction, walk mindfully through the experience, reason out solutions, analyze how those solutions are likely to work out, and take thoughtful, effective action.

Journal; In what areas of your life do you find yourself reactive? Are there times you wish you could have slowed your reactions, and been more able to think things through?

Learning Self Compassion; The negative self-talk is stuck in the amygdala in a self-destructive feedback loop. In other words, we are not even just reacting to _outside_ events, but more crucially, to this _internal_ self-talk. These negative messages trigger the fight, flight, freeze continually from inside our own heads so that we are literally stuck in our own _abusive relationship with ourselves_. So many people live in this internal hell and never know how to recognize it for what it is, and move through it to _self-compassion_.

In order to interrupt this negative loop, we need to take those early experiences that created these thoughts and beliefs, into our higher cortex so we can reason through them.

Notice your Narratives; It's not just what happens to you in your early life that gets stuck, but the _story or narrative_ you created about what happened. Most people grow up in some level of family trauma, dysfunction, chaos, etc. If your story about yourself is that you were to blame, you were flawed, unlovable, stupid, ugly, wrong, not enough, etc, you take those self-judgements with you into your life. Then every time you struggle, those self-judgements flare up like a forest fire, berating, harassing, belittling, and destroying yourself with mean messages. These stories are often created when we are very young and are the result of the thought processes of a very young child. Young children believe they are the center of their world, and so at that time, the things that are awful or confusing, seem to be our fault and are logged as such in our internal narratives. We reason that we are somehow flawed, wrong, not enough, ugly, terrible, unlovable, etc. The precious magical and irrational thought processes of a young child, tell us to make sense of the nonsense we are living in by making it our doing, and then we take those beliefs into the rest of our lives. As you answer these next questions, picture those experiences happening to *another* child and ask yourself if you would judge that child so harshly?

Journal: In very clear terms, what happened to you as a child that caused these harsh messages?
If you knew a child going through that, would you have empathy for that child?
What words would you use to love and support that child?
What messages about the child would you also share ("you were not to blame," "you were a precious child and not at fault," etc)
Spend some time saying those new truths and supportive messages to yourself and write about how you felt.

This is the beginning of _Self-Compassion_ and needs to become a daily practice; noticing when you are being harsh with yourself, recognizing whose voice, or what old narrative that represents from your early experiences, and rewriting the script to support yourself rather than berate yourself.
This self-compassion is a crucial part of your recovery since "you take yourself with you wherever you go." If you're in an abusive relationship with yourself, this must be your first focus, or you

will forever be miserable within your own mind.

These first pages of journaling can lead to months of therapeutic work. Take the time it takes to really work through this internal self-talk, change the chatter of your internal critic, and learn and practice self-compassion.

CHAPTER 2; FEAR, OBLIGATION, AND GUILT

Fear starts so subtly that we don't think of ourselves as fearful, or see our relationship as frightening. When you begin the relationship, you might even be aware that the person has a 'temper' but you tell yourself, 'they would never hurt me'. You don't recognize that being around someone who carries intense anger just below the surface, or blows up frequently, creates anxiety and fear in those around them. It also initiates a process of you trying to fix, placate, accommodate, and adjust yourself to prevent their anger. Violence, whether verbal, physical, sexual, or all of the above, does not happen out of nowhere or in a vacuum. It's part of this system of control, manipulation, and power. It starts subtly and gradually escalates over the course of the relationship. You also may be aware that they use just enough intensity or anger to get what they want; no more, no less, so that they teach those around them to keep them happy, or else. Since it all begins with love-bombing and other tactics to hook you in, they derail your rational mind, your red flags are buried by heart emojis, and yet they are gradually giving you messages about what's acceptable from you, and what is not. If you step outside of their wants, they will ramp up as much power, control, pressure, and aggression as needed to get you to back into your 'place,' and then they will love-bomb you again to let you know that's 'good behavior'. This cycle over time creates very clear parameters you intuitively know are ok, or not ok. When others in your life tell you you've 'changed,' you don't know what they're talking about. You're falling into the Fear part of the FOG.

Obligation; The sense of obligation develops over time with layers upon layers of manipulation. This is not only how you begin to feel obligated towards that person, but also often includes a sense of obligation towards their family members, friends, and even strangely, your own family and friends, or some vague sense of societal pressure. The societal obligations we put on ourselves are a heavy burden that we believe we *have* to carry. We think we have to continue a relationship that others think is good, or we need to be in a relationship because we are of a certain age, and if you're not, then something is wrong with you. We use these unwritten rules in our heads to force ourselves to settle and feel obligated to continue even a very toxic relationship. We often feel obligated after a period of time, to move in together, to marry, even when we have reservations or even deep concerns. Obligation plays a huge role in the FOG.

Guilt is the third part of the FOG and is intricately related to fear and obligation. The guilt is how you condemn and blame yourself for your fears and obligations. You not only blame yourself for *your* choices, but for the other person's feelings, moods, and actions, saying you must have 'made them mad' or 'stressed them out' or 'should have known they had a bad day at work,' or 'not talked to them about…'. When you guilt yourself for the other person's abuse of you, you are truly trapped in the fog, as you cannot see anything clearly anymore. You believe you are to blame, you have to change to suit the other person, and you grow more and more anxious and depressed trying to figure out how to do that. You are socked-in, have no bearings, no way in or out, wouldn't know which way to go if you did have a sense of the direction to safe harbor, and you have become disoriented and paralyzed in the fog.

Journal;
F; What have been the scariest incidents in this relationship?
What are the daily things, even small things, that bring you fear, anxiety, or stress?
Do you feel anxious, drained, depressed, upset, confused, or frozen a lot of the time?

Do you feel afraid of their temper? Anxious about their moods? On edge with their needs/wants/demands?

O; In what ways do you feel obligated to stay? Where did these feelings originate; society, friends, family, or this person?
Do you feel obligated to meet their needs? Do they tell you that only you understand them or can love them or help them?

G; How do they use Guilt to control and manipulate you?
In what ways are you feeling guilty for their moods, emotions, behaviors?
Do they tell you you're a terrible person/mother/father/friend/wife/husband/son or daughter if you don't do what they want, when they want?
Do they make you feel badly for wanting to spend time with others when they want you to spend time with them?

FOG; How do you feel about yourself within this relationship?
How do you truly feel this relationship has affected you?
How much do you tell the truth about this relationship to those you really trust and care about?
If you told your best friend or your closest family member the total truth, what would they say about how this has affected you, and what they wish you would do?

Recognizing the FOG and how it developed is crucial to clearing it out of your head. Let's first look honestly at the fear. The fear comes from the power, control, and manipulations this person uses on you. Time with this person sends adrenaline through your system every time you sense they may get upset with you. These are the signature tactics of an abuser and have nothing to do with you; there is nothing you did to cause them to be abusive, you can't control their behavior, and you will never figure out a way to make it stop. In Al Anon terms, the 3C's; you didn't cause it, can't control it, and you can't cure it. The only way to clear the fear is to get free of the frightening situation you're in. When you do, it will still take time to clear the fog of fear out of your system.

Journal; Can you recognize that you're trying to manage this person's behavior when it is clearly unmanageable? Can you list all the ways you've tried to make them happy, less moody, less angry, etc, and that none of it has worked?
Can you see that they have been this way all of their lives and that you didn't cause it, can't control it, and can't cure it?

The truth about Obligation is that there are NO obligations that supersede your safety, sanity and happiness. If all who care about you knew what was going on, they would be 100% supportive of you getting free. Anyone who is not supportive of you, is not a safe person to have in your circle, and needs to be given their eviction papers from your life. Societal obligations are in the same camp, but so often they only exist in your own head and have nothing to do with anything or anyone else. When you look at this sense of obligation, it's an internal self-judgment, and you need to learn to let that go.

Journal; What obligations are really just your own negative self-talk? What obligations can you recognize don't matter?

And the Guilt, ahh the guilt. We are only responsible for our Attitudes, our Awareness, and our Actions. We are not guilty for anyone else's moods, emotions, choices, behaviors, and never never never for their abuse towards us. Their abusiveness existed within them long before they knew you, and will exist in them after you are gone from their life. They will blame you, but their abusiveness is never your doing. So remember; you didn't cause it, can't control it, and you can't cure it.

Journal; What internal guilt messages do you carry? What new messages can you give yourself about your responsibilities and the many things that are *not* yours?

CHAPTER 3; TAKING STOCK OF THE ABUSIVE RELATIONSHIP

In this chapter, we will engage your rational mind to take stock of the facts of this relationship. We will explore how it started, what happened, and where you are with it now.

Let's start with the tactics they used to hook you in;

<u>Love-bombing</u> is when a person floods you with adoration in the early part of a relationship. You are 'the best,' 'the only one who has ever understood' them, 'the most amazing,' 'the most wonderful, beautiful, incredible person,' 'so above and beyond anyone else,' etc. The effect is to throw you off balance, to undermine your ability to keep your rational mind onboard, and to feed your emotional mind with the belief they cannot live without you, and you cannot live without them. This usually also has a flavor or 'it's you and me against the world' which tends to isolate you. Of course, real love can a little like this too, so how do you know if this is love or love-bombing? One way is to take a step back; keep your rational mind engaged, and don't let your emotions get too immersed too quickly. The narcissist or abusive person is all flash and crash, so if you slow things down, they will often either bail out of the relationship, or up their intensity and demands of you. If either of these happen when you take a moment, voila, you've got your answer! A *true love* that is emerging will have the maturity to allow you to breathe, to spend time getting to know each other, and to enjoy the process of seeing if you are a good fit and begin to grow together. If the person loses interest or freaks out and grabs onto you because you wanted to slow it down, you've dodged a bullet, and need to keep your distance. A sincere new love will not turn on and off like a light

switch, whereas a narcissist or other abusive person will. You might see them immediately attach to and love-bomb someone else, and that's a great indication they were love-bombing and not loving you.

<u>Mirroring</u> is when a person analyzes what you like and don't like, what you want and don't want, and even how you look and what you do, and then mirrors those things back so that you feel like you've met your 'soulmate' or twin. This, again, derails your self-protective rational mind, and causes you to fall into their control very quickly.

<u>Isolation</u>; As the narcissist or other toxic person senses you giving in to the love-bombing, and mirroring, the middle stage games begin. They will begin to carve you away from your interests, your priorities, and anything that gives you a sense of self and meaning. They do this to diminish *you* so that they can turn all of your attention to *them*. They begin putting down the things that you care about and wanting your time and attention all to themselves. They will be subtle or very blunt as they demean and devalue all that they initially praised and appreciated in you during the love-bombing and mirroring stage. As they begin isolating you from your friends and family, they diminish what defines you, and divide you from those who love and support you. As they put you down and control you, they don't want anyone in your corner building you back up or telling you to get away from this relationship. They will subtly put your family members down, or even say they think your family/friends are against them. They will insist you need to be on *their* team and not side with your family/friends. They may pick out insignificant conflicts between you and your family/friends and pit you against them. As you have less support, you are more vulnerable to their manipulations and their 'reality.'

<u>Devaluing</u> often comes right on the heels of these first tactics. Devaluing is when they run you down, pick on your flaws, tell

you that they love you 'despite' your many problems. They create the feeling that you are unlovable, but they love you, and they are likely the only one who ever will. This has the effect of making you feel unworthy, and it also makes you feel you need them and will never be loved by anyone else.

Gaslighting is a term that came from a 1940's play that then became a 1950's movie. It was about a man who was doing evil in the attic, which required he turn on the gaslights up there which would cause the ones in the living room to dim. When his wife would ask why the gaslights were dimming, he would tell her they weren't. Over time, he made her feel she was going crazy by continually denying these very basic realities she was perceiving. When a person literally denies reality, tells stories to make you feel like you're not in touch with reality, and makes you feel you're 'going crazy,' that's gaslighting. Anything you see, or say or want or need, and any perception you have, they will deny, degrade, or argue the opposite. This covers any complaints you have about their behavior, but ranges to the mundane as well. These games are designed to separate you from your sense of reality so that you lose touch with yourself almost entirely. When they deride you for even your most simple thoughts and perceptions, you lean into them for everything, and become more and more dependent. Sometimes you begin to feel so separated from yourself that you feel you're going insane.

Cycling: it's crucial to recognize that the way someone really nails down their control is through the cycling of these games. They hook you in with the love-bombing, then demean you with devaluing, while keeping you isolated. If you start to get sick of these toxic behaviors, they cycle back with some love-bombing. Over time the love-bombing is sprinkled in as mere breadcrumbs, but you start to live on these breadcrumbs as your only source of emotional food. The most damaging and bewildering aspect is that over time, they train *you* to devalue *yourself* and to begin to love them more for loving 'unlovable' you. You believe what they're saying, and feel worse and worse about yourself. You're so miserable, that you only feel a bit ok when you are with them, getting the breadcrumbs of "love" and attention they offer.

Devaluing yourself; As you devalue yourself, their work is done. You are putting yourself down, questioning your own reality, isolating yourself from others, and feeling more and more emotionally and physically bankrupt. You stay in the relationship for the breadcrumbs they throw out periodically, and they are free to get what they want from you when they want it, and to cheat and wander as well.

Endings; This can go on for years and years or it can end suddenly. There is no rhyme or reason; some abusive people keep their supply for long periods, usually out of convenience or to appear to the world that they are a good partner, or they tend to bounce to other relationships frequently. The relationship tends to end in one of two ways; either they find a new shiny object and move on, or you get sick of the abuse and decide to leave. If they discard you, they may still want to maintain control of you. Or they may find the new object didn't work out and they want you back. If you decide to leave, they will usually go all out to get you back under control, or punish you for daring to take your life back. This new set of games can be the most frightening and dangerous.

Aggression and bullying; It's crucial to recognize that an abusive person puts enough pressure on you to get what they want, and if you decide to leave, aggression and bullying, including violence, may very well intensify. The narcissist or other abusive person, when thwarted, goes into an emotional collapse, and may reach for anything and everything to get you back under their control. They may even vacillate between anger/rage, and tears/victim-stance. They may attack from victim-stance which usually sounds like, 'How could you abandon me!' Or they may just devalue you with; 'No one will ever love you like I do' 'You'll never be happy.' They will often cycle from rage, to collapse into tears, then fly into rage again. They may threaten suicide, which can be the most effective way to keep you trapped if you're an empathic person. The ramped-up aggression, and bullying reactions can be intense and dangerous.

Hoovering: If you've gotten away or they discarded you, but now they want you back, they may resort to Hoovering. This involves all the games they do to suck you back into a relationship (like a hoover vacuum cleaner). They will stalk you online, text out of the blue, or pretend they accidentally texted, and then try to engage you. They'll show up where they know you'll be, (at work or at school,) acting friendly and casual, but setting the hooks of manipulation to get you back. The charm will be ramped up, the love-bombing will be on again, and they may say they have changed, etc. Remember their breakdown is *not* a breakthrough and the likelihood of change is extremely low.

Flying Monkeys: When they feel they've lost and there is no hope of getting you back, they may show their true viciousness by sending in the flying monkeys. Most narcissists and other abusers have an entourage of "friends" they can rally to punish you. The monkeys will gang-stalk you on their behalf; insulting you, ruining your reputation, and tainting your friendships or relationships with family if they can. They will scheme a wide range of strategies to make your life miserable.

Journal:

Early on in the relationship, what did you notice about this person as they interacted with you, and others? Did you notice the love-bombing, mirroring, isolating, devaluing, and gaslighting?
Did you notice that you started to devalue yourself?
What do they do that makes you feel 'crazy'?
Did your sense of self and support from them vacillate wildly from feeling loved to feeling hated/disregarded/devalued?
What concerns did you have early on that you disregarded, or let

them talk you out of believing?
Could you see the cycling from love-bombing to devaluing, to love-bombing again?
In what ways are they aggressive, passive/aggressive, or bullying towards you and others?
Can you see how they zeroed in on your most vulnerable spots to use in their devaluing?
Can you see where your past insecurities, when shared, became their ammunition against you?
Can you see where they found your weakest self-perceptions, to focus their manipulations?
How were they dishonest?
What were the meanest things they did or said?
If there was an ending, how did they hoover, control, manipulate, or send in the flying monkeys?

<u>What do they mean when they say, 'I love you'?</u>

So many people are drawn in when an abuser professes love for them. If you're the kind of honest person who would never say, 'I love you,' casually, you likely take this very seriously when they say it to you. If they say it on the heels of a dramatic incident, or when you've had enough of their games and manipulations, you may think they've made a 'breakthrough', that they've changed, that they really do love you now. You may think they will be different, more caring and empathic. Or you mistakenly think you are 'the one' who can save the abuser, the one who has been missing all their lives, that you can make them treat you better than they've treated anyone else in the past. But here's the truth; when an abuser says, 'I love you' they mean one of two things, and neither one will turn out well for you!

Let's try to clear up some confusion; if you're an empathic, truthful, and genuine person, the behaviors of a narcissistic or abusive person just won't make sense. So, let's try to make sense of the nonsense that goes on inside them. Many say, 'abusers don't *have* feelings', but this isn't true either. What's very true is that they feel and process emotions completely differently from someone with empathy, and until you really understand that, you are at risk!

The abuser is like a hot air balloon, with an empty, fragile ego, needing a constant source of praise, adoration, and control, to keep the balloon inflated. Their sense of self and identity are dependent on others puffing them up, and when the supply lags or disappears, their balloon will implode and then explode. They lack empathy, feel they are entitled to get what they want when they want it, and to use and abuse others for their own will and desires. Their focus is entirely on themselves and getting their needs met, and the intensity of all of this is at a survival level. They will start with more subtle manipulations to get what they want, but can escalate all the way to tears, suicidal threats, rage, or violence. They can go from sweet to serial killer in a matter of seconds, and then back to sweet if you give in. They will literally make you feel crazy.

Understanding all of this, it is clear there really are only two things abusers truly mean when they say "I love you." 1) They are saying it to get something they want from you. Because they don't feel empathy, don't see your emotions, needs, or wants as important at all, and use and abuse for their own gains, they can easily lie, even about love, without hesitation or remorse. If you're not a dishonest person, you often can't even fathom how easy this is for an abuser, and you can get drawn in over and over again.

The second reason is more convoluted. An abuser feels their own version of 'love' when someone keeps their hot air balloon full, and never asks for anything in return. They feel what *they* consider love, and when getting their needs met, they may feel they've finally found, 'the one.' The problem is that they 'love' you as long as you are praising, adoring, meeting their needs and not asking anything of them. As long as you're excusing and forgiving their terrible behavior, enabling and placating them, and letting them be as toxic as they want to be, and not calling them out on it. This feeling of 'love' will dry up and blow away as soon as you lapse in your adoration, ask for any consideration for your emotions, needs or wants, or call them out for any using or abusive behavior. At this point, you will see their true colors as they implode, and then explode.

Many people get obsessed with and lost in the question of why someone would play all of these games, cause all this anguish, and keep doing it over and over even though it is so futile and seems so pointless. In a nutshell; abusers don't love, they take hostages. If you're 'in love' with an abusive person, you start to realize you are in it alone. Love has become a very confused and confusing term in our culture. In its most true form, love is a verb involving literal *actions* of caring for another person. Love–as a verb– means you are giving, attentive, that you actively care for another's thoughts, emotions, goals, dreams, passions, and that you are empathic towards them. Love between two people is a connection that enhances growth in each person. Each of you wants to be with the other, you want to take the time to get to know each other deeply, you ask questions and listen to the answers so you can understand them. As you understand them, you grow in respect for, and appreciation of them, and this is shown by your caring interactions with them. This is a fairly consistent experience and doesn't cycle from feeling good, to feeling terrible, and then good again. It progresses and deepens over time.

Narcissists and other abusers, by definition, lack empathy, are concerned only for themselves, their thoughts, feelings, goals, drives, passions, and thus, they simply *can't* create a loving experience with you. They can fabricate some of these emotions and actions to make it *look* like they love, but since it is fabricated, it won't be consistent. Their very nature is to want *you* to make *them* happy, to focus on them, care about *them*, to make *them* look good, and to puff up their fragile, empty sense of self. They want to be connected when they have a need; when it's good for their image, or their social media pics, when you can fill their loneliness or neediness. They are only interested in you as long as you serve *their* purposes.

They don't get joy out of seeing you grow your life. They don't take an active interest in what's going on with you; your goals, thoughts, feelings or what matters to you. If you find any new interests, they will be mad, annoyed, hurt, or aggravated. They will undermine any self-development you attempt, and belittle or degrade your emotions, wants, needs, passions, dreams, or goals. The truth is that they cannot 'love' because they lack the very skills that are required for love. The 'I love you' is cheap talk, while the actual walking the walk is impossible for them. They cannot 'love' you in any of the normal action-oriented aspects of the word. They will not be there for you. They will not stay true to you; if they have other desires, wants, or needs, they believe they are entitled to meet those, and will do so without remorse or regret. They may act regretful briefly if they get caught, but they are just upset their ruse is up, and that's not real remorse. They will not build you up, help you, care about your life, your growth, your passions, interests, dreams, or hopes. They literally are not interested and will let you know through devaluing anything you are into, and putting you down for wanting anything outside of focusing on them. You will continually feel that your world has to revolve around them, and you don't matter. You will feel as if the life is being sucked out of you, because it is; they need you to fill them, and will use and destroy you in the process.

So, when an abuser tells you they love you, or they can't live without you, they mean one of two things; they want something from you, or they believe you're going to keep their balloon inflated and they are saying it to keep the hot air supply coming. It's crucial that you recognize there is nothing in that arrangement that is good for you. They will decide when it's on, and they will decide when it's over. They will easily lie, cheat, and steal everything you have. They will bankrupt you emotionally, physically, spiritually, socially, and even financially. And when you're used up, they will kick you to the curb without a backwards glance.

Save yourself and your precious love for someone who can be loving towards you, in a caring, empathic, and reciprocal relationship.

Journal; How has this person used the word, 'love' to hook you and keep you hooked? What is real love, and did this person actually love you in the most action-oriented senses of the word? Seeing the entire relationship and this person as they are, can you really say you love and respect who *they* are?

Splitting is often called black-and-white, or all-or-nothing thinking. In a nutshell, it is the inability to see and manage all of the positive and negative qualities of yourself, others, and even life, and instead to split them into all good, or all bad. When someone uses splitting, they swing wildly between seeing themselves, others as perfect, to seeing it all as completely worthless. They see only the extremes; they use words such as 'always,' and 'never,' and will say things are either amazing, or it's all catastrophically terrible. They will gush with love, and then suddenly hate you. They can't tolerate anything but complete adoration from you, or they feel you're abandoning them. You often feel as if they pull you close, only to push you away again. Splitting amplifies every emotion and has a self-reinforcing quality. They often create their own dramas by insisting on extreme enmeshment in their relationships. They struggle to talk things through without their terror of abandonment flaring up, causing them to completely throw away the relationship. In healthier relationships we learn to accept all the strengths and challenges in ourselves, and others. We hold space for ourselves, and others to be human, fallible, and in doing so, we give each other space to be our whole authentic selves. Toxic people tend to split themselves as well as others. They attempt to stabilize their empty sense of self by seeing themselves as perfect, admirable, amazing, the best. The moment they stop idealizing themselves, they will crash into collapse and feel they are garbage. This implosion can then lead quickly to explosion. Of course. they will try to engage others to puff them up so they can return to aggrandizing themselves. If you don't, then you will be attacked as stupid, wrong, weak, ugly, and the most terrible person they've ever met. It's clear to see how splitting creates instability and dysfunction in relationships as they vacillate between defining you as all good when you gratify their needs and all bad when you frustrate them. You are idealized one minute and devalued or discarded the next. The wild swings look like mood swings and toxic people are often mistaken as Bipolar. They will furiously accuse you of 'always' doing the things they don't want you to do, and 'never' doing the things they want from you. These accusations are very disarming and degrading. They give you the clear message that you have to be perfect, or you are garbage to them. Their intensity during any conflict, and their demands that you do it all to their standard or suffer another berating, makes you feel completely devalued and lets you know that if you don't work harder to please them at all times, you are in the garbage category. You will also see them project these extremes onto others in how they praise and glorify anyone who supports them, and harshly judge and condemn those who don't.

Journal: In what ways did you see splitting in this relationship?
In what ways did you take these wild swings as your fault or about you being flawed?

Triangulation is a manipulation tactic where one person will not communicate directly with another person, and instead uses a third person to relay communication, thus forming a triangle. Triangles are also formed to create division and control between people. Toxic people are masters at the use of triangles to control, manipulate, and get their needs met. Some examples include; a parent engaging one of the kids to team up with them to isolate, bully, and gaslight their spouse. This parentifies the child, making them the 'surrogate spouse' to the toxic person. It completely disempowers the victim-spouse and empowers the toxic person.

The parentification of the child and the enmeshed relationship they form with the toxic parent is very unhealthy for the child and creates confusion of roles, relationship issues, and ongoing conflict with the victim-parent. Getting attention from a toxic parent is often so challenging that the child will welcome this enmeshment and go along with the triangulation, not realizing the depth and breadth of the manipulation and abuse involved. The victim-parent will be undermined in their parenting, and feel more and more depressed as they feel unloved, unwanted, unneeded, and misunderstood. Ultimately, this can lead to the complete despair that fuels suicidality. This is a deadly and destructive triangle that is very common in families with a toxic parent. Another example is when an adult child triangulates one parent against the other. This also creates conflict, destruction, and despair as the family is torn apart. Triangles of any origin can lead to long term estrangement in families. When everyone talks directly to each other, they may be able to identify the toxic family member who has created these divisions, and the family can be reunited. If you have a family division, go directly to each person and see if there hasn't been a manipulation by one family member to divide the others. Life is too short to allow these things to fester and take on a life of their own.

In romantic relationships, triangles are often used to create jealousy, and intensify adoration. When a toxic person is first love-bombing a new victim, they will often play them off of a real or imaginary rival. They will talk about their past partners or someone who was flirting with them, to stir up competition and jealousy. This often pushes a new victim to have sex sooner than they might have or let the relationship progress even though there were red flags. It may spur them to work harder for the abuser's attention, giving the abuser a huge hit of adoration. The swinging back and forth from love-bombing to triangulation is part of how they draw you into their web. They dangle the love-bombing to entice, and then triangulate to control. These are some of the strongest foundations of the trauma bond.

Triangles are also used to gaslight you. The toxic person will engage and use others to help solidify their story of events to make you feel crazy. They may do this when a victim is getting sick of their abuse and trying to regroup to get out of the relationship. They will let others in on the 'conflict' in their relationship but spin it to make them look like the victim, and make the victim look abusive or crazy. They will act like a martyr and talk about what they've had to 'put up with'. They will get friends and family to side with them, and make the victim look like the problem, or 'overly sensitive' or 'too much drama,'. Others may buy into this and try to 'help' while only fueling the abuse and making the victim feel more alone and desperate. They will continually use these triangulated conversations to support their version of reality, telling the victim, 'Everyone agrees with me.' This triangulation creates a powerful force to isolate and disempower you. You may even try to talk to everyone about the truth of the situation, but the fog of the abuse makes it hard to combat this type of gang-gaslighting.

Journal: What triangles were created and how did you respond?
Did you feel isolated and gaslighted by these triangles?
Did you feel that you must be wrong since they had rallied others against you?
What can you see now is the truth of the situation and how can you stay focused on the truths to help yourself get emotionally and physically free?

CHAPTER 4; BELIEFS, BEHAVIORS, ATTITUDES, AND ATTRIBUTES OF TOXIC, ABUSIVE AND NARCISSISTIC PEOPLE.

As I said in the beginning, we're not going to focus on labels or diagnosing abusive people, but this next section is a synopsis of the beliefs, behaviors, attitudes, and attributes to help you identify what hit you, and what to stay away from in the future. There seems to be a myth that a covert narcissist is a gentler, milder form, yet let's imagine you're a soldier and you and your unit are in a war zone. The enemy has two sets of folks out to get you. There are the overt ops; the bombers, the troops, the artillery. And then there are the covert ops; these guys are stealthy, scheming, cunning, and surgical in their strike. They are the masters of disguise, they make a strategic plan, and when they hit you, you're caught completely off guard, completely by surprise, and you're done.

A covert narcissist or abuser is no less *dangerous t*han an overt one. In many ways they are *more destructive* to your sense of self, your sense of safety, and your sense of sanity. A covert will hunt you, hurt you, and hold you hostage so stealthily that you will be blindsided by it. When you've been with a covert, you're generally more baffled by what happened, and live in denial much longer. You can't believe you misjudged them so seriously. Often others in your life don't see them as abusive at all, so you have a harder time reality-checking with family and friends. Others may even have bought into their manipulative stories and are blaming you for all of the negative happenings in the relationship, and too often, you're not even sure yourself what went wrong.

Where the overt tends to be outwardly grandiose, aggressive, self-aggrandizing, exploitative, and have extreme delusions of grandeur and a need for attention, the covert tends towards smug, passive-aggressive, disdainful, contemptuous, vengeful, and scheming.

Whereas the overt exaggerates achievements and talents, the covert tends to act out in false humility. They will even act in self-deprecating ways to manipulate you into complimenting them. They are very self-absorbed and are hard pressed to engage with others in any meaningful way, as all conversation focuses on them. They tend to be preoccupied with fantasies of unlimited success, power, beauty, brilliance. The covert will not often share these outwardly as an overt will, but internally, this is still what drives them. They believe they are special or unique people who can only associate with other special, unique people. This comes across as condescension towards others, contemptuousness, smugness, and distance. They don't have deep friendships or relationships, and they only stay connected as long as there is something in it for them. They think others are stupid and beneath them, and not worth their time and attention. They will often engage in a passive/aggressive flavor of this being the 'misunderstood special person.' This gains attention through getting others to feel sorry for them and seeing them as victimized or abandoned. Others often fall into this and don't realize until later that the covert has created all of their 'abandonment' by driving others away with their behaviors.

They require excessive admiration; this is usually manipulated in passive/aggressive ways such as playing the victim, sullenness and silent treatment if you spend time with others; or smoldering anger when you don't give them the attention they demand. The covert has a buffet of strategies they use to get attention, and when others get sick of adoring and admiring them, they will flip things and demand they be doted on because they are sick, injured, upset, or otherwise overwhelmed.

They have a sense of entitlement, believing that others should comply with what they want, when they want it. The underlying belief that the world does and should revolve around them, drives much of what they do to get their wants and needs met. When they're not in control, heads will roll! The covert is more prone to use punishing silent treatments, passive/aggressive sarcasm, playing the victim, and other implosive acting out. They are exploitative, using others for their own needs and wants. Relationships with others are for the sole purpose of taking what they want to benefit themselves. They will pour on the charm, shower with compliments, and build you up so they can take everything you have to give. When you are used up, or they find a new shiny object, they will coldly cut you off and toss you out like last week's garbage. They will trash-talk you, find some small fault to expand and over react to, cover their tracks with cruel lies, twisted stories, and gossip to undermine you so their own viciousness is not so obvious.

They lack empathy, meaning they are unwilling to recognize or identify with the feelings and needs of others. The covert will often feign empathy, offer cheap lip-service of concern for others, while their actions make it clear they have no concern with and no feeling for anyone but themselves. When a person lacks empathy, they also lack guilt and remorse. They can put on and take off emotions like they're changing clothes; they'll put on sadness, maybe even tears to show others they are not monsters, but underneath they feel no empathy, no guilt, no remorse.

They will blame others for their issues, problems, and even their actions. "Look what you made me do!" is a typical response after they have done something terrible to you.

They are envious of others and believe others are envious of them. They are in constant competition and often create imaginary measuring-up wars. They use gossip, scheming, and other underhanded ways to win at all costs, even when others are not aware they are competing.

They show arrogant behaviors and attitudes, which can range from smug eye-rolling, contempt, that tells you they think you are beneath them, and you're not worth their time, or energy.

They look down on, make fun of, and talk negatively about others continuously. They only feel good if they can make others look and feel badly.

Of course, there are other types of toxic behavior that don't fall under the narcissistic traits.

The emotionally vomiting one; this person often sees themselves as the victim in every circumstance. They continually bombard you with the drama of their lives to the extent you feel overwhelmed. Sometimes you start as a compassionate friend for them, but later realize they are not seeking to move forward into a new chapter. Any positive suggestions are not needed or heeded, and you feel like your time and efforts to help are wasted. You realize they are continually wallowing in this stuck place; looking for sympathy and to be coddled. Although compassion and caring are obviously important in relationships, this is not that; this person wants you to rescue them; and over time you realize that is just not possible. In this person's presence you often feel exhausted and depressed.

The gossip; this person talks down about people constantly. You might notice that this is their primary or even their only source of conversation. At first you feel special because they build you up while running others down, but eventually you realize you're probably the source of their put downs when you're not there, And for sure, you're right!

The angry one; this person is chronically angry at the world; they hate their boss, their job, their spouse, their siblings, their neighbors; it doesn't matter, they are angry and venting all the time. Initially you think you're valued as the person who supports their difficult life, but eventually you realize their anger has an addictive quality and they seem to love their venting! You often feel down after hanging out with them as this toxic anger is very draining.

The sickly one; hypochondriacs are another form of toxicity and being with them means listening to the endless details of their ailments. Often you initially have compassion for them, but later realize this is a chronic condition of their *emotions*.

Of course, we all are sad, sick, frustrated or needing to vent sometimes, but toxic people are this way *all* the time and suck the life out of you with their needs. They rarely let up, and they never offer any reciprocity.

Journal:
Which of these behaviors resonated most when thinking about the toxic person in your life?
Which of these behaviors did you think were your fault? Can you see now that they are not?
Are you exhausted by this person? Does time with them suck the life out of you?
Do you often wish it was over but not know how to make it end, and fear the repercussions of ending it, more than the drain of staying?
Are you suicidal; feeling like that may be the only way out?
Do you wish they would find someone else but you feel so unlovable you also fear that if they left you, you'd be crushed?
Are you becoming isolated, depressed, confused, feeling unlovable, unworthy, and notice it is getting worse and worse over time?

Of course, there are vast gradations of manipulation, control and abuse, and for some of you, setting firm solid boundaries will be helpful, and you may be able to learn to stand up for yourself within this relationship. For others, getting out is crucial for your safety and sanity.

For some, armed with this radar-reality, you can make a wise decision and move out, move on, and start to heal. For others, this is not the case. Let's unravel why.

CHAPTER 5; TRAUMA-BONDING;

Healthy love and bonding is the normal process of growing a sense of love and care for a person through shared experiences, trust, being present, and knowing, and feeling known. Trauma-bonding results from the cycle of abuse, in which someone seems to love, know, and care for you, but then abuses and devalues you, creating dependency, confusion, and self-condemnation. You believe if you somehow 'get it right,' the abuse will stop, and you will only experience the positives in the relationship, and thereby your very sense of self, and sanity are torn down over time.

And you feel like if you leave them, the loss would be devastating. This feeling is real but is because the unhealthy bond causes your amygdala to react as if your very survival depends on this person's presence in your life, when rationally, you can see that this person is destroying you.

If your rational mind can assess all of the above and say, 'I don't want to be with someone like that,' but you still find yourself pulled towards them, you're struggling with an unhealthy attachment, dependency, or a trauma-bond. While *rationally* you can see that this person is destructive to you, you still feel *irrationally* pulled into their orbit.

<u>10 Questions to Assess Your Trauma-Bond;</u>
To find out how trauma-bonded you are to this person, here are 10 questions to ask yourself;
1. Do you take responsibility for this person's behavior; berating yourself for not being perfect, and justifying the way they treat you?
2. Do you strive to get 'back to how we used to be'; believing the love-bombing person is the real person, and thinking this angry, mean person is your fault?

3. Do you say things to yourself like, 'Well I already have too much time invested to quit now,' thinking that you need to stay because it's too hard to leave, and that if it were right to leave it would 'feel' right?

4. Do you want out, but are afraid they will become more dangerous and frightening if you leave? In truth, an abuser's behavior *is* more unpredictable when you leave, so this is a good reason to create a *safety plan,* but *not* a good reason to stay.

5. Do you keep thinking that if you were better, smarter, taller, thinner, fitter, fill in the blank, they would be faithful, nicer, kinder, more decent, or less angry at you? Remember, abusive character qualities are innate in *that person*, and are NOT dependent on anything you are doing or not doing. A person is honest, nice, kind, decent, faithful, and able to handle frustrations without anger, blaming and demeaning you, because that's who *they* are. And conversely, a person is dishonest, mean, abusive, demeaning, unfaithful, and angry because that's who *they* are. Neither one is your doing.

6. Do you feel emotionally, physically, socially, and even intellectually bankrupt? Do you feel you've always had so much to give and felt good about who you are, but now feel you have nothing and are nobody?

7. Do you believe no one else will ever love you so you might as well stay with them? Do you worry that you have become so boring, depressed, and anxious that no one could or would ever want you?

8. Do you find you hate yourself more and more over time? Do you hate the way you look, walk, talk, think, dress, or feel, and can't see anything good about yourself?

9. Do you live for those rare, brief times when you get some positive attention from this person, and try desperately to figure out how you got those moments so you can replicate your efforts and maybe 'finally get it right' so they will love you again?

10. Do you sometimes have fleeting thoughts that if you died that would be your way out? Or do these even progress to genuine desires to hurt yourself? (If you answer 'yes' to this one, please call

the suicide prevention line in the Introduction to this book!)

If you answered yes to any of these questions, you're trauma-bonded to this person. The more 'yeses' indicates a higher intensity trauma-bond that is covering more internal ground. And unfortunately, this is more accurately described as 'bondING,' because it's not something that happens once, but it continues until you make it stop. The longer a bond continues, the harder it is to break. You will become more and more bonded over time, more destroyed internally, and less and less able to get yourself free.

<u>Journal:</u>
What questions most ring true for you?
Write about all of your thoughts and feelings while reading this list.

CHAPTER 6; PLACATING, PEOPLE-PLEASING, AND PEACEKEEPING;

One thing we really have to address within ourselves is the self-designation as the placater and peacekeeper in all of our relationships. We often have developed this tendency in childhood and need to realize in adulthood that this is not our job. We are responsible for ourselves; our attitude, awareness and actions. We are not responsible for other's emotions, their attitudes, moods, actions, or choices. Often in the process of trauma-bonding we have taken on such a fully engrossed role of placating and peacekeeping that we feel lost and empty when not over-enmeshed in someone else's emotions, moods, and choices. This codependency is how we keep being toxic to *ourselves* even when the toxic person is out of our lives. People have recently begun to refer to this as 'fluffing', or 'fawning' the abuser, and these are apt terms. But let's be real; fluffing, placating, fawning and peacekeeping are manipulative. You are essentially zeroing in on what the toxic person wants or needs and giving them that supply for the purpose of getting what you want from them. Some therapists on Youtube have even advised this as a short-term strategy to 'downgrade the power of the narcissist,' to 'placate and calm them, to satiate them for a time.' Although I understand the rationale, I think this is ill-advised and dangerous.

When I see clients fluffing instinctively, this is the first thing I want to encourage them to STOP doing. When you are raised with an abusive parent or are involved in a relationship with an abuser these are natural *survival* responses and have probably helped in your survival to some degree. As a child this was probably smart on your part, and you need to let yourself recognize this and even give yourself a pat on the back for figuring out how to survive your childhood. But as an adult, I never want someone to continue these strategies. This fluffing, placating, people-pleasing, and enabling, ends up emboldening, and empowering the abuser, and essentially perpetuates your own self-degradation. You're disempowering yourself and continuing the cycle of their tantrums. You're enhancing your trauma-bonding and solidifying your own perspective as the victim.

In this relationship, you have likely found yourself noticing every nuance of their mood, and emotion, and obsessively trying to make everything perfect to keep them happy and prevent them from being upset. This response is a normal reaction to their behavior, but it's also what creates your own stress reactions, and overall self-destruction. Understanding this relationship dynamic is crucial to getting healthy within yourself and not allowing the abuser to control you, your emotions, and your life.
Let's take a deep look at this cycle; abusers want what they want when they want it. They are like a hot air balloon that needs to be pumped up continually, or they implode, and then explode. As long as you are pumping, they are ok; as soon as you stop, look out! As their stress increases, their voice changes, their pressure on you becomes more focused and intense. You can feel in your body that you are beginning to react; you feel more tense, more anxious, panicky, upset. You begin to feel trapped, and dread what's coming. If you've been in this relationship a while, you may notice you respond in fight, flight or freeze. Often the next step is that you begin to frantically start fluffing or placating. You might try to do something or say something you think will shift their mood and emotions. In your desperation to placate their emotions, what are you sacrificing? In a nutshell, you're losing your entire self. When you focus all of your attention on another's emotions, moods, and all of your energy on managing their moods and emotions, you're losing touch with your own. You're also busying yourself to make them happy at the cost of doing things for yourself. When the placating 'works' temporarily, you may breathe a sigh of relief, but then the process just starts over,

and you find yourself in a continual cycle of stress, placating, relief; stress, placating, relief. When this becomes your life, the costs can become profound. We know that chronic stress destroys your immune system, tears down your emotional and mental health, and programs you to be laser-focused on someone else's well-being, while neglecting your own.

If, despite your fluffing or placating efforts, the abuser explodes into a tantrum, with rage, or tears, threats towards you, others, or themselves, they will often emotionally tear you down, showering you with insults, degrading you, devaluing you, and destroying any sense of worth you may have for yourself. They will often blame you for their behavior, saying that if you had done this, or hadn't done that, you would not have upset them so much. In this blaming, they refuse any responsibility for their emotions or behavior, pressuring you to accept it all. This usually causes you to then tear yourself down internally. You blame yourself, feel you maybe should have done this, or not have done that, and if you can somehow do things differently, then they will not be upset, and all will be well. You often commit yourself to further placating, and deeper levels of self-degradation, and self-denial. Over time this causes you to bury yourself deep in the muck of this dynamic.

Often at the end of a blow up there is a honeymoon period. The calm and warmth is so welcome after the storm, that you will do anything to keep it going, so you push yourself, your emotions, needs, and wants, deeper into the abyss, closing yourself off even more profoundly, as you fluff and placate more.

<u>Journal;</u> In what ways did you take the role of placater or peacekeeper in your early childhood? In what ways have you placated, fluffed, enabled, and empowered the toxic person? What has been the effect, over time, of this dynamic?

<u>Boundaries;</u>
If there is a way to get free and go no contact with a toxic person, this will ultimately be healthier for you. But if that's not possible,

here are other strategies;

The emotional maturity of this person is very limited. In many ways it is helpful to look at this behavior as if you're dealing with a 3-year-old's tantrum, but this is happening in a larger, scarier body. As we talk about how you take care of yourself in this process, this perspective will be our touchstone.

When a kid tantrums it's because they didn't get their way. Your job as a parent is to give them appropriate boundaries to help them grow and mature. You know they have to tantrum sometimes to test those boundaries and you have to ride out the tantrum without giving in. You know you have to stay calm, not engage in their fit, and hold solid boundaries. You know not to take anything they say or do personally, to stay the course, not to throw anger back at them, and not to think their fit is your fault. You know that placating a tantruming child is to invite more of that behavior. So even though it's hard to ride out the screaming, you put them in time out, breathe, self-calm, and walk away.

In dealing with an abuser, you need the same perspective to help you protect yourself from the emotional destruction. When you see that this is a fit born of not getting their way, you can see that their tantrum is not your fault. It's not something you did or didn't do, but is only their reaction to a reality they don't like. Placating or fluffing them is not healthy or helpful to your sanity, or even their growth. When you placate, you lose yourself, and also deny them any opportunity to look at the truth of their actions, the reality of the boundary they are fighting, and realize that they are responsible for their own emotions, reactions, and responses. When you stop taking responsibility for their emotions and reactions, you won't feel so deeply damaged by them.

What does this look like?

1. Stay in your own skin; don't let yourself get carried away into their emotions. Stay present within yourself, check in with yourself. If you're getting anxious around that person, breathe, and self-calm.
2. Do not think it is your job to take care of or calm them;

it's not and it only makes you sick to engage in that thinking.
3. Resist the temptation to do any placating or fluffing. This is natural and instinctual, but it isn't healthy. Fluffing might allay your anxiety in the moment, but in the long term, it keeps you enmeshed with them, and destroys your sense of self.
4. Give them a grown up 'time out' by walking away, driving away, or hanging up the phone. You can say something or not say anything, it's up to you.
5. If you want to say something, make it short, clear and concise; 'I can see this is not productive, I'm going to hang up now, (or leave, or go for a drive, or take off.) You can call me when we can have a calmer conversation.'
6. Realize that when you do this, your anxiety will initially *increase*. You will feel afraid of what they will do and what they will think and feel, and this will be your focus. Breathe, calm yourself, and remind yourself this is important, and you need to take care of you, not them.
7. Consciously disengage from them and their roller coaster of emotions, and focus on yourself. If they begin to escalate again, be a broken record; keep saying the same thing and keep the boundary. You can further say, 'I'm not going to let you talk to me that way. We can talk when you've calmed down.'
8. Finally, Remember the Al Anon slogan; you didn't cause this, you can't control it, and you can't cure it. You may even need to say it to yourself over and over in the beginning. It is *their* job to mature to a place where they take care of their own emotions. If they can't or don't want to, that's fine, but you're not going to participate in any way, and you're not going to allow yourself to be trashed or enmeshed.
9. If the escalation is violent, call 911 immediately. Don't feel guilty, and don't feel you caused the escalation. All you did is start to live healthy boundaries and refuse to

be used and abused. If they escalate to violence as a result, that was there all along, just under the surface.

Being with an abuser is physically, emotionally, and mentally devastating. When you engage in fluffing, placating, peacekeeping and enabling, you are further caretaking and focusing on them, which keeps you in that instinctive survival mode, makes you sick, and helps them stay in denial and immaturity. You can keep yourself safe and sane through healthy boundaries and self-care. It's tough at first and your anxiety might initially escalate, but over time, having good solid boundaries is empowering, relieving, and gives you back your life.

Journal:
There may be many areas of your life where you engage in people-pleasing with friends, family, coworkers, and within the toxic relationship. What would happen if you stepped away from the peacekeeping role and started to notice and take care of your own emotions, attitudes, awareness, and actions?
In what areas of your life can you try the above boundary-setting? Write about those here.

PART 2; GETTING CLEAR

CHAPTER 7; C IS FOR CLARITY

When the fog lifts off of the ocean and you can see again, the feeling is euphoric relief. The sky is bright, blue, open, and you can see for miles. Your heart stops pounding, you're no longer disoriented, confused and terrified. You can regroup, set your course, and continue on your journey.

I settled on the acronym CLEAR to talk about how to emerge from the fog.

<u>C; stands for Clarity;</u> When my husband and I bought an old sailboat in Ventura, California a number of years ago, I was looking at the sails, the hull, the auto-pilot, the lines leading back to the cockpit, the beautiful old teak rails, the teak cabinetry in the cabin, the galley, and even the two-tone teak cabin sole. I wanted to know how she sailed, how the engine ran, where they'd sailed her, and how she handled the wind in light or heavy air. My husband is a licensed captain of ocean-going tugs. He navigated up and down the west coast, and to Hawaii and back for over 30 years, and knew little about sailing at the time. His main focus was safety, and he was simply ecstatic the little 31-footer had radar. He knew that fog is one of the most dangerous aspects of being on the ocean, and he would not leave the dock on this or any boat unless we had radar. Even though radar merely gives you green lines on a screen, showing you outlines of the coastline, with flashing dots that warn another ship is bearing down on you, it's enough to help you chart a course, and move forward. In a thick fog, you have to put your trust in the radar, which is scary, but so much better than having no idea what is around you at all. When my husband showed me how to read the radar in our old sailboat, it was fascinating, but imagining using those squiggly green lines and blips to orient and navigate through dense fog was

not really much of a comfort. As you journal, you are beginning to develop what look like lines on a green radar screen. You're getting some bearings and sense of the coastline and dangers around you, but it still doesn't look like a clear horizon where you can see blue sky for miles and breathe a deep sigh of relief. As you're starting out on this journey, it is tough to trust these lines and blips, and take action to navigate in the right direction. Just as in our sailboat, you will struggle to trust this radar-reality, and believe it enough to move out, move on, let go, and begin to take care of yourself. But just as on the screen, this IS reality; the dangers, and the route to shore *are true*, and you need to begin to trust these realities as you chart a course towards safe harbor where you can start to heal and rebuild.

Your *radar-reality* has begun to take form in the *facts* you've developed through the first part of this workbook. Though it looks vague and it's scary to chart a course, learning to see these facts for the safety they provide, and to *trust them*, is crucial to navigating a way forward. Your radar may have begun from your own glimpses of truth that hit you after a serious episode, or your friends and family telling you the truth, or your own fleeting thoughts saying this relationship is unhealthy, toxic, or abusive. It can look like these green lines of wanting to get out, even while believing you can't. It can even take the form of suicidal feelings, believing that killing yourself is the *only* way out. If this is a thought in your mind or a feeling in your heart, this is a serious warning that you are in a very unhealthy situation. Often soon after these realizations happen, you get sucked back in with the manipulations, blaming and shaming yourself, accepting their fake apologies, which can unravel your resolve and put you back in the fog. So as this radar-reality takes form, grab onto these facts, and write them down in your journal. These facts will help you make healthy decisions, chart a course, and make a move forward.

Journal;
What are your new radar-reality realizations? Write out these

facts and recognize that although they are blurred and fogged by your feelings at this point, the facts will be very important moving through this process.

Clarity means taking an honest inventory of this relationship, the toll it's taken on you, the isolation, the damage done, the lack of reciprocity, the reality of how drained, sad, and anxious you feel. Your primary relationship should be where you recharge and rest from the hectic world around you. If this is not the case, if your relationship is where you find the most stress, the most pain, the most confusion and upset, there is something wrong.
Coming to terms with who that person truly is provides some solid green lines on the radar to help guide you out of the fog.

<u>Journal:</u> In looking at all of what you've written so far, what would you say is a healthy course through the fog? Do you need to get out, go no contact, or learn and use healthier boundaries to keep yourself safe and sane?
What would you say are this person's real character qualities; not what they *claim* as their values or character, but what you *see* in their behavior that *shows* you who they really are? Someone can say they value honesty, integrity, compassion, empathy, family, friends, time together, etc. But what do you *see*? You can see someone's values in their actions. Specifically, where do they spend their time, talents, and treasure? Do they value you and others with their time? Or do they spend their time obsessing on money, appearances, social media, trying to look good to others? Are they wasting their lives on meaningless things like video games, TV escapism, or other addictions? You have to learn to accept what you *see* and not what they *say*. How do they spend their talents? Are they pursuing any dreams, goals, passions, something they care about? Or are they focused on making themselves look good superficially?
How do they spend their treasure? Where do they spend their money? Is it wasted, obsessed over, or put into valuable use?
As you take stock of this person, do you *want* to be with someone

with these character qualities?

Learning to see a person's character through their actions, and not believing blindly in their words, is part of the radar-reality. 'Talk is cheap', is the truth. Fully embracing this truth will help you sort through this experience much more thoroughly, as well as help you avoid people like this in your future.

When you've been manipulated and abused by someone, or many someones, you begin to not trust anyone. But you can learn to weed out those who are trustworthy from those who are not and learn to trust YOURSELF. The vague green lines on the radar have given you the reality you needed to begin to see the abusive relationship for what it is, and as the fog lifts, you will see the scene around you in three dimensions and full color.

CHAPTER 8; L IS FOR LEAVING;

When you recognize with Clarity, what is really going on in this relationship, it's time to leave. For some this is literally leaving, going no contact, but for others, (whether due to shared custody of children, or if this is a parent, or sibling or for any other reason you have to deal with them,) this is about *emotionally distancing* from them to regain and retain your sense of self, sanity, and happiness.

Facts vs. Feelings; At this point it is essential to see the difference between the facts and your feelings. We've talked about the reactive mind and the rational mind, and now it's crucial to see that the way this plays out is that you may still *feel* love for this person and yet, *decide* with your wise mind that this relationship is not good for you. You can decide to leave, while still feeling you love them. It's a decision you make, not necessarily a feeling you feel. In our culture we put a lot of stock on our feelings, and much emphasis on a "follow your heart" philosophy. If you're in an abusive relationship you must NOT follow your heart because it's been jerked around to the point of becoming trauma-bonded to this person. You literally cannot distinguish between 'love' and this unhealthy trauma-bond. You have to step back and look at the relationship *rationally* and you have to follow your *wise mind*. This is a decision, often against your feelings, so don't wait; you can love and leave.

You also need to realize that the cycle of abuse is seductive. Often in an abusive relationship there is a cycle; a build-up of tension, an explosion of some sort, and then a honeymoon period. Because the honeymoon period feels good, people are often drawn back into the relationship over and over again. In the process, their emotions are becoming more torn down over time, until they forget what a normal, non-drama life feels like.

When you make the decision to leave, you'll notice this love feeling will occasionally still want to draw you back in, to seek that honeymoon period feeling again. Remember *reality* and don't allow your heart to derail your head. In this you have to let your wise mind have the last word. When you get tempted to see that person or talk to them, just don't. It's like a drug and you're addicted; one bit of contact can lead to another entire cycle of abuse. It's not worth it. In addiction recovery we teach people to think it all the way through. This means to think through to the awful conclusion before deciding to take that first step back into the addiction.

Leaving is clearer when you realize that your *reactive/emotional* mind is trauma-bonded to the abuser, while your *rational* mind is not. You know with your *rational* mind that you are in an abusive situation and are trauma-bonded, you can make the *rational* decision to get out. Of course, as you do so, your *emotional/reactive* mind will quickly spin into frantic desperation to reconnect with the abuser. Keeping the *rational* decision front and center, supporting, and having compassion on your own *emotional reaction*, but staying the course through the process of disconnection, will get you free emotionally as well as physically. It might help to bullet these steps and strategies;
1. Recognize that the FACTS are separate from your FEELINGS; Trauma-Bonding means that it will never *feel* right to leave. When you recognize this, you can *decide* to leave, and then follow through, no matter how your emotions try to pull you back in. You recognize it's the right thing to do for you and your well-being, and you walk through the process with this truth as your radar-reality. You may still feel love and you may still *want* to stay, but in your rational mind you know that person will never change, they will not treat you right, you are not at fault, and you don't want to live this way. You have to keep these FACTS in the forefront and treat the FEELINGS as just emotions that will gradually heal.
2. Let the *Facts* steer your ship. Since you've written out all

of the facts of this relationship, let these journal entries help keep yourself on track, no matter what your emotions say. Managing these two parts of yourself can be like having an adult and a tantruming child living inside your head. The rational adult knows you need to get free, while the emotional child is escalating, frantically trying to reconnect. The emotions may feel overwhelming, out of control, even survival-level intense at times. Steering your ship based on the radar, means focusing on the North Star of freedom, staying the course, riding out the storm of tantruming emotions inside, knowing there is sunnier sailing ahead. This is very confusing, and often feels impossible. Be assured, the emotions will pass. But realize if you comfort your emotions by reconnecting with the abuser, you start steering into the storm and fog again. The abuser may love-bomb you to get you back, and then they will again tear you down, and the trauma-bond will become even stronger. It will take time, but if you steer straight through the storm and fog, the tantrum inside your head will ease and finally cease. Keep the facts and feelings clear and separate and keep the rational mind stronger than the emotions.

3. Realize that NOW is best. Trauma-bonding increases, intensifies, and internalizes over time, so the longer you stay, the harder it will be for you to get free. Your emotions will tell you that you should stick around and see if it works out. Your emotions will say that you've got a lot of time invested so you should keep at it. But the longer you stay, the more bonded you will become. You will lose more of yourself, internalizing more of the negative self-talk and self-degradation, and you will have dismantled more of your reality. So, the old adage about ripping the bandaid off quickly is a good analogy; once you decide with your rational mind to go, NOW is the best time.

4. Reach out for support; you need a therapist, or a friend or family member who knows you well and can help you keep your feelings and facts straight. Be brutally honest with them. You might even want to share your written facts, so they know all of the truth of this relationship. Ask them for honest feedback. Often, they have been holding back on what they see in your relationship in order

not to hurt you. Assure them you now want them to be really blunt and direct. Walk them through your new understanding of trauma-bonding and how you know you need to get free even though at times, you don't want to. Let them know how to help you stay on course through the storm of emotions that will come, and how to challenge you if they see you getting drawn back into the relationship.

5. Recognize the dangers involved. When you reclaim yourself and your power, you should anticipate that person's reaction, and take a realistic assessment of the dangers, if any. They may have a "narcissistic collapse," imploding and then exploding, or they may coldly walk away like you never existed. If they collapse, this may involve everything from tears and suicidal threats, to rage and violence. Have a safety plan that includes calling 911 if suicidal threats or violence erupts. Do not go this alone and do not feel badly about calling the police if they escalate to that point. If they walk away, your emotional mind will desperately want them back. Make sure you have thought these things through and talked through every scenario with your support person or network.

6. Realize the abuser has gathered a massive arsenal of ammunition to manipulate you. They have studied you and managed you and your emotions over the entire time you've been together. When they lose you, they may use all of this to maneuver you back under their control. The love-bombing, cycling with devaluing, gaslighting, and other strategies will be ramped up and intensified. Be ready! It's best to minimize or block all contact if you can, and if you can't, make sure you commit to new boundaries so the abuser cannot work away at your emotions and manipulate you back into the trauma bond.

7. Recognize how you've enmeshed yourself in them. This is baffling, and for many it convinces them they're 'really in love' and then they go back to the abuser. Your emotions have been so enmeshed that you may feel anxious, empty, and desperate to know what they are doing, thinking, feeling. You may find yourself desperately wanting to reconnect, and obsessed with getting them back. If you realize this is part of the trauma-

bond, and know this will happen, you can prevent yourself from being drawn back in. Why do you feel this way? You've literally spent months or years reading the abuser's every emotion, mood, and attitude, and guessing at their every want or need. You've so intertwined yourself with them that you've ceased to exist in your own personhood. You are completely wrapped around them in every way. The moment you sever contact, you become like a junkie needing a fix. You may even find yourself lying to your support people to try to get back in touch with the abuser. When you see your emotions wanting to take you down this rabbit hole, stop, ask for help from your support people, realize this is normal, and recommit to getting free. Engage your facts vs feelings realizations again and walk yourself gently through this detox period.

7. Trauma-bonding is worse for those who had abusive childhood experiences. Studies show that if you grew up with childhood trauma, you will be more likely to trauma-bond with an abuser. This happens when the abuser's devaluing statements seem familiar to you, or if you already believed similar lies about yourself. They hook you by finding the broken, hurt spots in you, and pushing those specific buttons to make you feel terrible. As they find and push those old buttons, sending you backwards into old hurts, they can use and manipulate you more efficiently and effectively, and cause you to self-abuse more easily. Thus, if the negative berating resonates with old messages from childhood, you will need to heal those old wounds as well as the present ones.

8. Recognize that it's just as hard to let go of the internal trauma-bond if you were discarded. If you're now free of the relationship because the abuser ended it, you will likely feel very distraught and tell yourself you "weren't good enough," or some other nonsense. It's crucial to recognize that they likely attached to you because you had so much to give, and they are getting rid of you because they have completely bankrupted you emotionally, physically, spiritually, and socially. They will now move on to their next target. You need to step back, take this time to recover, heal, and rebuild your life. Many spend a lot of

energy cyber-stalking their ex to see who they connect with, and then feeling even worse when they see them immediately start a new relationship. The self-degradation continues with all of this new ammunition against yourself. If you're doing this, Stop! Disconnect from them; recognize they will do the same thing to that person and try to be grateful to be free of them. This starts with refusing to listen to the irrational emotions of wanting them back, not buying into their story about how useless, worthless, or unlovable you are, and beginning to heal the other hurt spots inside with your new self-compassion. In addition, don't delude yourself that because they discarded you, they won't reconnect. They may very well contact you when you least expect it and will possibly destabilize you just as you are gaining traction in rebuilding your life. I've known people to get drawn back in by a casual text just as they were feeling good about themselves. And sadly, they went on another cycle of abuse as a result.

9. Give yourself the time it takes. Just as your body lets go of the need for a drug over time, you will gradually release the hold of the trauma-bond. The craving for the emotional connection to the abuser will gradually leave you, and you will learn to self-support rather than self-abuse. This requires that you spend time changing your internal self-talk, and spending time with supportive people. Remember the underlying abusive personality disorder doesn't readily change if ever. IF the person wants to change, you still need to separate from them emotionally and physically and let them do that work themselves. Don't stay with them while they figure it out. Recognize that continuing with them is too destructive to you, and it's a long hard journey they need to undertake themselves. Take good care of yourself and use lots of self-compassion to help love yourself back to good mental health.

<u>Journal;</u>
List out the FACTS of this relationship; did this person enrich, expand, and care about your life, or shrink, isolate, and destroy your sense of self and your life? Did you feel safe, loved, helped,

or made to feel degraded, anxious, depressed, and ultimately destroyed?

List out your FEELINGS in this relationship; do you still feel love for this person? Do you still feel anxious when they are not there? Are you afraid you will be empty and lost if you leave them or they leave you?

Write out your decision about what's best for you; even if you know you need to while you still don't want to.

List support person/people

Map out your safety plan if you need one

Have you shared the truth with them and asked for them to be truthful with you?

Emotionally Leaving; The Journalist Method:

If you have to stay in contact with this person, you'll need to learn to set healthy boundaries and to emotionally detach. I used to refer to this as taking notes, like an anthropologist, but I've realized it may be more helpful to call it the Journalist Method.

Think about a journalist in a war zone; I'm always amazed at how they can be totally present, completely intrigued and completely unflappable. When a journalist goes into a situation, they are there to do a job, to gather information, and stay focused on the facts. They remain solid and steady no matter what is going on around them. They may need to break down later, but not in the moment while on camera. Honing these journalist attributes can help you navigate the minefields of dealing with a toxic person. Let's walk through one attribute at a time.

1. A journalist stays focused on the facts. Let's say you're meeting your ex to pick up the kids. The facts are the time, and the place, and if you can stay focused on these and nothing else, you will navigate it well. Don't let them pull you into any other discussions or conversations. When you stay focused on the facts, you can get in, get the task done, and get out without getting drawn into an emotional minefield.

2. A journalist stays disengaged and doesn't take anything personally. When you're dealing with a toxic person, they will try to draw you in by attacking you personally. Remember these are their own issues and none of their stuff is about you. You've been on their train tracks and been hurt many times before, so stay off the tracks. It's not about you, so take nothing personally. Notice it all in your best journalist demeanor and just say to yourself, 'interesting.'
3. Be intrigued, not involved; observe, don't absorb. A journalist is intrigued by everything but is not rattled by it. So, notice everything, the games, the manipulations, the attacks, the various attempts at control, notice how they can flip from tears to anger, to putting you down, to building you up. Notice it all, learn from it, watch it as if from behind your notepad. Be intrigued and again, just say to yourself, 'interesting.'
4. Marvel at the madness. Be amazed, rather than devastated by the madness. Simply say to yourself, 'wow, they actually just said that, or did that, or attacked at that level in that way.' Marveling from an emotional distance helps you not to personalize.
5. Flatten your affect. The journalist keeps a flat affect and does not react throughout the interview. They never let on how they feel or what they think. The benefit of this is that a toxic person who is trying to rattle you, engage you, and manipulate you, feeds off of your reactions like a shark feeds off of blood in the water. When you react, you create a frenzy of activity for the shark, whereas complete non-reactivity confuses and disarms them. Some people call this the 'gray rock' method; being as interesting as a gray rock.
6. Journalists don't argue with their interviewees. No matter what the opinions of the person being interviewed, the solid journalist never engages in arguing, justifying or defending their point of view. In

the same way, realize that arguing has never gotten you anywhere with this person, so stay focused on the facts, get the task done, and realize anything else simply fuels the toxic person.

7. Journalists take notes but don't keep score. Manipulative and toxic people want to engage and to win. But it really does take two to tango, and they have to engage you emotionally in order to get that win. The only way you win is if you don't engage. Take care of yourself with self-compassion, and supportive self-talk. Only then do you emerge unmoved, and unscathed. Just notice, keep your emotional distance and physical safety, and that's your win!

8. Journalists are not there to have *their* stories heard. When you're dealing with a toxic person, sharing *anything* about yourself will only make you vulnerable, so don't talk about how well or how poorly you're doing, how awful or awesome it is to be away from them, or tell them that others are mad at them too. Don't say anything personal at all; be a journalist. Taking a pot shot, trying to make them feel angry, guilty or sad, may be tempting in the moment, but you will rarely get the response you want, and you will often reignite the flames of envy, frustration, loss of control, and other reactions that will be impossible to tamp down. Don't light that fire. Stay focused on the facts without sharing anything about yourself.

9. Though we never see it on camera, I'm sure the journalist falls apart after they get off camera and out of harm's way. In the same way, it's crucial that you take care of yourself *later* when you are out of direct contact with the toxic person. It's normal that you will come away from this experience with a lot of emotions; you may need to cry, journal, talk with your therapist, friend or family member. Take care of yourself, do healthy things to let off steam and to detox from the experience.

You can't let it out in the moment, or you'll emotionally engage the toxic person. Just know you're going to take care of yourself later. Vent out all of the things you kept yourself from doing or saying in their presence, in your journal or to your support people. Self-care and self-compassion are key. Realize this is hard, completely out of your comfort zone, and feels impossible. But handling your difficult relationships this way will help save your sanity.

So be a journalist; a strong, solid, unflappable, tough, laser-focused journalist.

Some additional things to remember when standing up for yourself; They are, by definition, wholly self-centered. They want what they want from you and are not concerned with your well-being. This means you have to be super aware of your well-being when interacting with them, including remembering what you want, what you need, what your boundaries are, and your values. The abuser will drag you across every boundary you ever thought you had, and you will be so blind-sided you won't see it until it's done. Stay very aware of yourself and your well-being. They lack empathy. This means they are not aware of or concerned with your emotions, so you have to be super aware of your emotions or you will get lost and depressed while around them. Since they will love-bomb you one moment and attack and degrade you the next, it is challenging to keep your emotions stable and intact. Remember they take care of themselves and not you, so you will not get their approval or high fives for taking care of yourself; more likely you will get their ire and anger. As you learn to step back and emotionally separate yourself from them, recognize you can be strong and ok even in the midst of their games. Learn to witness the scene, watch the circus go by, watch their games and marvel at the manipulations, while not letting them impact you. You may even anticipate their next manipulation and see it for what it is; seeing them flip from drama, to anger, to devalue, to love-bomb, to triangle, etc. Build more people into your life; do not think you will ever get anything back from this relationship; at best you've only ever gotten breadcrumbs. If you have to be in relationship, then so be it, but don't think they are your friend or companion or that you will get any validation, support or love from them. Feed your life and yourself with your own self-compassion, and others who are empathic and caring.

In summary, learn to step back, watch the drama as if you're separate from it, take care of you, and don't take any of their manipulations personally.

Leaving can be physical if you can move on and not spend any time with the abusive person, but if you have kids together or you work together or the abuser in your life is your parent, adult child, or your boss, you may have to learn to cope with them. These critical coping strategies will help you maintain your sanity and sense of self, in essence leaving emotionally, even though you are still physically around them.

Journal:

Write about emotionally separating even if you have to remain in some sort of contact with them. How will you tell yourself their actions are about them and not you? Which of these strategies did you find helpful, surprising, and how will you incorporate them if you have to be around your toxic person?

Grappling with Grief: Leaving, whether emotionally or physically, will create an ending of sorts, and at this stage, it's ok to let your emotions flow, supporting yourself with your support people, and your new self-compassion. You've experienced loss, and you will need to allow yourself to grieve. Your sadness may be more for what you had *hoped* this relationship would be, rather than what it was, so be aware of this as you grieve. But there also may be real losses involved; not getting to see your grandchildren if you separate from your adult child, losing family members of the ex-partner, leaving friends behind who sided with the abuser, losing a home, a beloved pet, a lifestyle, etc. Don't let your emotions pull you back to the abuser; just let yourself feel. Hold safe space for yourself while you experience the sadness and let yourself know 'this too shall pass.' Many people believe that if they let themselves *feel*, they will be overcome and overwhelmed and 'never stop crying.' Yes, it *feels* that way, but the *fact* is that spending some time allowing the myriad of emotions, clears them away so that you are able to free yourself from the past and experience new emotions.

Back in 1969 Elizabeth Kubler Ross wrote the book, On Death and Dying, where she coined the famous "Stages of Grief." Later in her life, she noted that the stages are not a linear and predictable progression. Her later works corrected the first by saying that the stages are *phases* we wander through, revisiting each of them, back and forth, as we gradually work our way through our grief. The phases she and other clinicians identified are;

<u>Denial or Refusal to Understand</u>; In this phase, you often believe the loss is somehow a 'mistake', and you cling to a false reality. You might experience numbness and you may think, "I just can't believe it."

<u>Anger or Resistance;</u> When the reality lands on your heart, you'll often feel frustrated, or angry, especially at whoever is closest to you, thinking, "Why did this happen? It's not fair!"; "How can this be?"; There is also some angry blaming and hostility towards those seen as responsible.

<u>Bargaining</u>; This phase involves the hope that you can avoid the grief by doing something differently to change the situation. Often this will trigger you into hyper-placating mode. Sometimes this looks like negotiation or 'if i had just..., this wouldn't have happened.' This can be a dangerous phase as you may talk yourself into reengaging with the abuser.

<u>Depression or Catharsis</u>; In this phase a sense of despair and hopelessness can settle in. You might isolate in this hopelessness and feel it will never end and never get better. The catharsis is the pure grieving part where you cry and cry and begin to release the denial, or bargaining, and just cleanly grieve.

<u>Acceptance or Integration</u>; In this phase you begin integrating the loss and finding ways to cope and move forward. You may feel calm, pensive, and find yourself in a more stable condition of emotions.

Notice yourself weave through the phases; feeling disbelief, shock, anger, sadness, despair, revisiting disbelief, and then some integration. You can be triggered and start back through disbelief, despair, and anger again.

Grief is like ocean waves coming up on shore; they are big and stormy at times, knocking you over and making you feel like you're going to drown. Then they recede for a while, only to be triggered by a song on the radio, or a birthday or another event, and a big rogue wave washes over you again.

The important aspects of this image are several; that you will feel better, and then worse, and then better again. Don't despair when a rogue wave hits you, just think to yourself, 'this too shall pass.' When a wave hits, you are not back to square one, you are just experiencing a wave. When you remember and encourage yourself with these truths, you will weather each storm more productively and with less fear and despair.

Avoiding grief makes it grow! Grief that goes unresolved can lead to mental, physical, and sociological problems and contribute to family discord. Grief gone underground is a terrible thing; have you known someone who just stays angry after a loss? They are in grief that got stuck.

Complicated grief can happen if you feel guilt or any other complicating emotion. If you find yourself getting stuck, find ways to unpack the complicated emotions, and purely grieve.

Recognize that the three-month mark is very tough and often people feel they're "supposed to be over it." Also, recognize that every holiday and significant date; birthdays, anniversaries, etc. may be risky times.

The truth is, we may need to cry a lot to get through some grief.

Oftentimes you need to take it just one moment/day/or even

one breath at a time; there's a song called, "Just Breathe;" and sometimes that's the best you can do.

Realize that new grief brings up old grief; don't be surprised if old sadnesses come up because of the current situation. Honor all of your grief and don't shame yourself for your emotions.

Take care of the basics first; make sure you are sleeping, eating, taking care of your basic responsibilities.

Take care of yourself or you can't help others. Often when you're going through something hard, there are still people relying on you; kids, parents, work colleagues. Try to balance taking care of yourself with keeping track of your other responsibilities so that you don't feel you are losing your entire self/life/everything.

Compartmentalize; it may be good to go to work and focus on other people and other things for some hours a day. But then give yourself time and space to fall apart.

Journal;

Write about your emotions, your grief, what you've lost, what you imagined this relationship might be that you have to let go of.

If your grief is getting stuck, ask yourself if you're complicating it with guilt or other baggage? Are you stuck in the denial, bargaining, anger, depression phases?

Write about periods of some relief, or moments of acceptance and integration of this experience.

Can you see yourself beginning to see this as a learning and growing experience from which you will heal?

CHAPTER 9; E IS FOR EDUCATE

When the fog lifts off of the ocean, you look all around you to see where you are and decide where you're heading next. Developing this complete picture of your situation is vital to finding your bearings and moving forward. We want to be people focused on always learning, growing, and expanding our outlook. In the FOG we shut ourselves down to anything but survival. Being in the CLEAR means we open ourselves up to new possibilities. We become curious again, excited about our lives, able to imagine new experiences, new activities, and even new people. When you emerge from an abusive relationship, it's good to educate yourself about what happened so that you won't fall into that trap again, but don't stay stuck immersing yourself in learning about abusive relationships. Learn about healthy relationships and learn about completely different things that have nothing to do with relationships. Take a class, join a club, learn a new sport, activity, or restart one you lost while immersed in the abuse. Learning makes us feel alive, intelligent, capable, and engaged with ourselves, others, and the world. It takes our perspective from the narrow survival mode and expands it to the stars.

Journal; In what ways have you felt your world shrunk, and in what ways can you now expand it? What do you want to educate yourself about? How can you focus on the positive possibilities, not the negative past? This new beginning is all yours. You are the writer, the director, the casting director, and the star of your new movie. Since you've just left the set of a real horror show, it's crucial you intentionally create your next film.

What kind of movie do you want to create? How about a grand adventure? A travel movie? A comedy with loads of really smart, funny people? A movie about self-exploration and intrigue? And maybe later when you've healed a bit more; a rom-com!

Write about things you've wanted to do, to experience, and to create; then embrace the exuberance of creating it the way you want it to be.

<u>My Empathy is Killing Me!</u>

One area of educating yourself needs to be how to stop attaching to toxic, narcissistic, or abusive people. How can you stop falling into relationships where others manipulate you? How can you see them for what they are and stop trying to rescue and help them? How do you maintain your empathic self, and see through the masks of others? You *can* learn and practice good boundaries. You *can* be empathetic without becoming a victim.

The term "empath" came about in a Star Trek episode, and has come to mean those with strong empathy, high emotional intelligence, and strong intuition. It also seems to have taken on negative connotations of being seen as easy targets for narcissists and other abusive people.

Are empaths magnets for narcissists? Short answer: Yes. But we can stop being targets without losing our strong sense of empathy in the process.

You'll find lots of different explanations of empathic people; here's mine; Empathic people believe in others, see the best in others, empathize deeply, care intensely about the well-being of others, and tend to be genuine and honest with most things, except with their own feelings, needs, and wants. Empaths can't comprehend that there are people in the world who don't care, don't empathize, don't feel as deeply, don't see the best in others, and don't believe the best in others. They want people to think well of them, they value being there for others, and love to feel needed. They prefer to help others, rescue others, and make others the center of attention, rather than to be helped, supported or praised. They feel terrible if they hurt someone, whether intentional or accidental. They have a deep sense of meaning and purpose and cannot understand superficial obsessions.

It's obvious that the empathic person is a perfect set up for falling into a relationship with a narcissist, or toxic person.

The narcissist needs their fragile ego bolstered and the empath wants to make everyone feel better.

The narcissist needs to be the center of attention and the empathic person is uncomfortable as the center of attention.

The toxic person lies, cheats, steals, and then adamantly stands by their denials, or gives shallow excuses, while the empath believes the best in others, and lets these things go over and over.

The narcissist is self-centered, the empath is other-centered.

The abuser will hurt you and then blame you for it. The empath is quick to blame themselves, to feel terrible when they hurt others, and will want to make the abuser feel better. This is why the empath is easily manipulated back into a relationship when the narcissist expresses hurt or abandonment.

The empath wants to rescue others; the abuser won't take responsibility for themselves, so needs to be rescued and enabled. The empath doesn't often see manipulations for what they are. They feel deep empathy even for a narcissist in collapse. In rescuing the narcissist, they form a deeper and deeper trauma bond with them.

The empath often doesn't see how anyone could be dishonest, cruel, mean, manipulative, self-centered, or intensely disconnected from any empathy for others. This leads them to be easily caught up in the stories and lies. The empath simply doesn't believe even the facts right there in front of them. When the abuser blames them for "making me mad", the empath readily sees the episode as their fault and strives to do better. The empath may see the truth for a moment, but if the toxic person expresses upset, sadness, hurt, or abandonment, or if they challenge that truth with their own gaslighting version, the empath will jump right back into relationship with them out of empathy, caring and wanting to see the best in them.

It's a perfect fit and a perfect dance for the abuser. It leads to stronger and deeper trauma bonds over time, and to the empath falling into depression, anxiety, and eventually to complete breakdown. The empath's sense of self is destroyed, and since the abuser has systematically isolated them from friends and family, they are at serious risk.

So, If you're an empathic person are you doomed to attract toxic people? Sadly, Yes. An abuser is going to be seeking someone who will be all of these things to them, and will hone right in on someone kind, caring, selfless, and willing to accept their bad behavior and keep on giving and giving until they are all used up.

But just because an abuser is attracted to you, doesn't mean you need to fall for them. You can be an empathic person with a great creep-o-meter, and great boundaries. How do you do that?

1. Keep your wise/rational mind on point when you meet people, and keep your deeply empathic self, protected behind the rational mind. This means that when first getting to know someone, be a journalist; ask good questions, listen, and gather information about this person as impartially as possible. Don't let your emotions get carried away before you truly understand what makes this person tick.
2. Know and accept in your deepest, innermost being that there are many people in the world who are not nice, not honest, who lack empathy, will hurt you, control you, and destroy you for no other reason than they felt like it. AND you cannot and will not fix or rescue them. Many toxic people are so keyed in on how an empath's heart and soul work that they will play the injured puppy in the road just to get the empath hooked.
3. You're looking for a partner NOT a project; if you feel hooked in, and feel moved to help or rescue, or to be the one that gets them to finally commit, and finally have a good loving relationship, RUN! What you're feeling is not love, and this is not relationship material.

4. Keeping your wise/journalistic mind on point, look more deeply into a person, noticing things like arrogance, bravado, vindictiveness, meanness, even in their mildest forms.
5. Ask yourself questions like; Does this person tend to laugh at other's pain, do they enjoy making others upset or hurt and then sharing that with a group to get others to laugh? Do they like being online trolls, and cyber-bullies? Are they demeaning, flip, arrogant, rude, and insulting to others, even the server or busser at the restaurant? Do they take up all the oxygen in the room; needing to always be the center of attention? What happens when someone else tries to get a word in, or tell a funny story; do they encourage and share space, or do they grab the attention back to themselves? Are they a know-it-all, telling others about their achievements, and do they disconnect and express no interest in anyone else's experiences, point of view, input? Do they tend to make others feel stupid for adding something to the conversation? Are they vengeful when something happens that upsets them; telling you about how they got back at, or got over on someone, and do they get puffed up and excited as they tell you how they made someone else hurt? Do they talk negatively about others continuously, bonding with you by tearing others down?

When you see these things in a person, you know they are not relationship potential. And because you've been in your journalist or wise mind mode, you have been able to gather this information and make this assessment BEFORE you got your emotions involved with them. You can now keep these *facts* clear and not let your *feelings* get drawn in by the lost-puppy-in-the-road act they may put on to lure you in.

In summary, you can be your empathic self, AND see the whole picture clearly. You can care deeply, believe the best, AND see through the shallow façade of the toxic person. You can realize that being needed and rescuing others should happen in your volunteerism or work life, not in your most primary relationship. Your primary relationship should be where you gain refuge and nurturance; where you recharge and share your day. Your home should be a place you feel joy, safety, love, and acceptance, where you share empathy with another empathic person. If those things are not true, you have a project, not a partner, and you need to cut ties, get free, and move on with your life.

Journal: Do you see yourself as an empathic person? What qualities do you see that you love and respect about yourself? Can you see how these make you attractive to a toxic person? What strategies from above can you use to change the way you interact with people so that you are no longer the supply for toxic people?

Developing a Trustworthy Creep-O-Meter: and the one thing that will make it malfunction!
Another critical area of self-education is how to protect and defend yourself powerfully so as not to get drawn in by another abusive person, ever. Many people do this by becoming a recluse, or being the bitter, detached scowling person, or the person who gives off an f. u. vibe when you get within 10 feet of them. But genuine self-protection comes from looking at the red flags you ignored and getting honest with yourself about the times you knew there was something wrong but you squashed your own wisdom and intuition. When coming out of an abusive relationship, many ask 'how will I ever trust someone again'. I tell them, 'I hope you won't; I hope you'll learn instead to trust yourself!' Trusting yourself is the only way to keep yourself safe. How do you learn to trust yourself? You have to develop a trustworthy creep-o-meter.

Developing a solid and trustworthy creep-o-meter, that redlines when you're around an abusive person, strengthens you from the inside out. You learn to trust yourself, your wisdom, and your intuition. You don't have to recluse, be bitter, or defensive; you can be yourself, trust yourself to know a toxic person when you meet one, to respond by setting boundaries, and by taking care of yourself.

There are several components to this so let's break it down. First, remember there are two different aspects of your brain you can use to gather information from others that will help you assess your safety with them. Start from the perspective of the rational mind; when you meet someone, ask yourself what do you see, what do you hear, and how do you interpret these things? People give off physical signals about who they are, including their posture, their body language, their eye contact, and proxemics. Proxemics means how close they stand to you, do they respect personal space, crowd you, pressure you, and overall, how do they present themselves? Listen to what a person talks about; including what they say, do they listen, what are their interests, activities they engage in, what are their life goals, how do they talk about their friends, family, work colleagues, supervisor, the wait staff, or the busser, do they talk about showing up for others, including their family, friends and even acquaintances and strangers? Next, how do you interpret this information with your rational mind? Taking all of this data and analyzing it objectively, what would you say are this person's core values, character qualities, and attitudes. Are they an empathic person or a user/abuser? Do you see and hear a person who values compassion, caring, listening, honesty, diligence, hard work, empathy, humor, as well as being humble, able to learn, and grow? Or do they show that they value self-centeredness, arrogance, cutting corners, doing the bare minimum, cheating others, getting over on, or getting revenge on others, burning bridges and moving on without looking back, cruel sarcasm, harshness, rigidity, meanness, and vicious gossiping? If you assess at this point the person is the second bunch of character qualities, log that information, and *do not let your emotions get involved with this person at all.*

Your emotions or reactive mind are the part of you that is more easily duped. Your empathy may get hooked, and may make you susceptible to others' manipulations, as soon as they start shining you on, making you feel special, and engaging other games to throw you off of the reality that your wise mind has already concluded; that they are this second bunch of character qualities. Let's say they fall into the first category of positive character qualities. You can now feel safe enough to engage the intuitive/emotional part of you. This involves asking yourself how you feel around the person; do you feel comfortable or anxious; do you feel you have to impress them, or do you feel you can be yourself; do you feel like you're talking to an old friend, or doing a job interview; do they seem open or closed when sharing about themselves; are they are genuinely sharing or playing games? Do you sense they genuinely want to get to know you or are they all about themselves? Do you feel a sense of comfort in their genuine care and compassion for others, coming from them? Do you feel embarrassed of their rude or condescending behavior? Do you feel sorry for those they are talking down to, or sharing negative stories about? Do you feel comfortable sharing your thoughts, feelings and ideas, or do they put you down for your ideas, rigidly holding to their own and unable to even listen to a difference of opinion? Do you feel inadequate around them? Do you feel they genuinely learned something from their last relationship? Do they take ownership of some of the things that went wrong, or do they trash their ex and blame everything on them? Do you sense they have a humbleness, an ability to take things in stride, an ability to laugh at themselves, or at least not take themselves too seriously all the time, or are they projecting continuous bravado, where if anyone pops that balloon, they will implode or explode? Overall, do you feel cared about, valued, interesting to them, important to them, or do they leave you hanging, make you feel you're lucky to be with them, or like you're not that interesting or important? Do you feel respected? Do you feel they are interested in your character and values or something else? Do you feel they are pushing you into a relationship, or honoring what you want? Do they make you feel that if you don't do what they want, they will take their attention elsewhere?

Putting all of this information together, from your wise mind and emotional mind gives you what you need to keep yourself safe. You can ask yourself at the end of an encounter with a new person, where is this person registering on my creep-o-meter? Is it in the low creep zone, the medium, or is it redlining in the extreme creep zone? If it's medium or redlining, set good boundaries and steer clear. If it's low, then maybe you want to learn more. What are your concerns? Honor them; step back; take your time. What's very true is that you can fool some of the people some of the time, but you can't fool all the people all the time. So, when you slow things down, spend time with this person, meet their friends, family, and continue to grow your information about them, they will show more of who they are. It's easy to fall into a relationship, and so hard to pull away and repair the damage if it turns out badly. If it's real and good, it will be even better if you give it time to develop.

So, what is The *one* thing that will make your creep-o-meter malfunction every time? Sex. Plain and simple. There is a chemical substance that floods your brain when you have sex and it's called oxytocin. We refer to it as the "attachment" chemical because It's the same substance that floods a woman's brain when she breast feeds a baby. Amazing right? When you have sex with someone, you're at risk of attaching to this person with the intensity of a mother and baby! And yet it is common in our culture to have sex with someone before you know very much about them at all. Let that sink in for a moment. Most people have a 'third date' expectation, that if you like each other at that point, it's time to have sex. Instead, what if you waited until you knew and trusted someone enough to give them the keys to your house, car, and the PIN number to your debit card. Sound radical? Well, if you don't know them well enough to give them access to these 'valuables', do you really want to give them access to your most precious valuables; your heart, your body, your intimacy, and your attachment? In conversations with clients, listening to horrible, abusive interactions with a partner, I'll ask what keeps them in the relationship and they'll answer with true conviction, "I really love" him/her. Sadly, what they're feeling is this oxytocin high, combined with the results of the trauma-bonding, and nothing else. This is not love. When we walk through their rational, and emotional assessment of this person, they can see this person does not have the character qualities they are looking for, does not have the values they want in a partner, does not treat them well, is not loving or caring, and makes them feel terrible in so many ways. But they keep coming back to the statement, "I love them". That's attachment, trauma-bond, or even addiction, but that's not love. So, if you want to have a strong and trustworthy creep-o-meter, you've got to keep your wise/rational mind on board by keeping sex out of the picture until you've really gotten to know someone. If you've fallen prey to someone already, and you feel this 'love', step back and recognize what it really is. Check in with your rational and emotional mind; engage your creep-o-meter, and you'll be better able to see and get free.

In summary, having a solid and trustworthy creep-o-meter is all about what you see, what you hear, how you interpret these as the person's values and character qualities, and how you feel when you are with this person. Don't let sex into the picture too early or you will derail your growing knowledge and be at risk of bonding into an unhealthy relationship. Trust yourself, and you will learn to consistently take care of yourself and steer clear of narcissists and other abusive people.

Journal: What are your thoughts about using your wise/rational mind first to learn about a person? Have you disregarded your wise mind's concerns in the past, and gotten involved emotionally and physically? Can you see how you've let yourself be drawn into unhealthy relationships by having sex too soon? Can you make a new commitment to yourself about this?

CHAPTER 10; A IS FOR AWARENESS

As you emerge from the fog, you will experience a new awareness. You will notice the positive things, people, and experiences that had been lost to you in the fog, and also the negative old beliefs and patterns that need to be relinquished. This is a spring cleaning of old habits, stuck attitudes, and old beliefs about yourself, and a reinstalling of your more positive self-awareness. This can be a challenge if you carry a lot of self-deprecation, self-hatred, or self-criticism. We've talked about this since the beginning of this book, and it's an issue that may need to be revisited over and over as you practice self-compassion. The new Awareness is in how you see yourself, talk to yourself, how you treat yourself, and how you focus on your life and future. As you move forward, focus your awareness on how you envision feeling good about yourself and your life.

Journal: What are some ongoing self-messages, self-condemnations, and other self-deprecating statements that you need to expunge? Going back to the beginning chapter on learning self-compassion, what are the self-supporting statements you found? Bring those forward and create new ones to continue this work on self-compassion and self-forgiveness.

Forgiving Yourself

Your compassion for yourself likely needs to start with forgiving yourself. You may not realize you are harboring unforgiveness, so pause for a moment, and see if you have been angry at yourself; are feeling 'bad,' 'wrong,' or 'stupid' for getting into or staying in the relationship with the toxic person? Forgiving yourself means realizing you did the best you could at every point in time. You tried to make things work, to believe in someone, to see the best in them, to be forgiving of them, and to trust them. Unfortunately, they were not believable, remorseful, or trustworthy, but that doesn't make you bad, wrong, or stupid, it means that person is unbelievable, untrustworthy, self-centered, and abusive.

So often this process of sharing your story, getting help, and getting free, causes you to run into crushing self-judgment for getting into and staying in this relationship. The internal voice calls you self-deprecating terms for staying as long as you did and trying as hard as you could. But let's look at this more objectively. The reasons people stay highlight some genuinely positive character qualities within themselves; qualities such as, Commitment, Loyalty, Determination, Believing in someone, and being Forgiving. These are wonderful qualities when shared with a healthy, empathic partner. In fact, they are essential and admirable, noble, gracious, and positive. They define you at your most core self and show who you really are. Forgiving yourself requires that you see this reality; that the qualities that kept you there are good qualities. Supporting and nurturing yourself in this internal conversation is crucial for two reasons. First that you stop thinking you were 'stupid', and instead see yourself as the loving, caring, loyal, forgiving person you are. And second, that you recognize that throwing away these qualities in the future is not what will keep you safe and sane but developing a better creep-o-meter is all you need. What's faulty in your creep-o-meter? You tend to believe people who are not telling the truth, trust people who are not trustworthy, and have empathy for people who have no empathy for others. When this happens, you are setting yourself up for heartache, trauma-bonding, and another abusive relationship.

Journal;
Do you beat yourself up for having stayed in the relationship?
What do you say to and about yourself inside your head? What is the truth of why you stayed and tried? Can you see these are good qualities that will be wonderful when shared with a person who

also has these qualities?

<u>Forgiving Others; Vengeance, Resentment and Forgiveness;</u>
Vengeance is a popular rant these days and it's shocking how many people dwell on and fantasize about what they'd like to do to get back at someone for hurting them. We live in a culture bent on revenge; but when you brew and stew about getting over on, or getting back at someone, you are literally poisoning yourself from within. Resentment is the quieter version of vengeance and takes up just as much valuable space in your mind. Forgiveness feels weak, and seems like it communicates acceptance of what happened, making you feel even more like a victim. But let's look at the reality of these three things and how they really play out in your mind.

Everyone has heard the analogy that holding a grudge is like drinking poison, hoping the other person dies. But do you REALLY get how truly poisonous this is? When you dwell in anger and resentment, you are flooding your system with stress chemicals. These chemicals have now been shown to cause a depletion of the immune system, literally depressing the helper cells that keep you from getting everything from a cold or flu, to possibly cancer. This stress chemistry has been shown to cause damage to your cardio-vascular system, leading to increases in blood pressure, strokes, and heart attacks. And this stress chemistry creates a cortisol build up in your brain, which causes depletion of the serotonin, endorphin, and other positive neurotransmitters, leading to or exacerbating depression and anxiety. So to say you're drinking poison, is not an exaggeration.

In addition, stewing in vengeance and resentment keeps you hooked into the person who wronged you. Have you noticed that when you're planning your revenge, when you're dwelling in the wrongs of others, you're angry and frustrated and that's all you think about, talk about, or fantasize about? You're renting free space in your valuable mind for that person and their wrongs. How much space and how much time have you spent rehearsing angry conversations, vendettas, and vengeful plans? How much more do you want to give that person? Sadly, many people give up a lot of space for many years and are largely unaware of its impact on their lives.

Third, you undermine future relationship possibilities by being rooted in the past. Have you ever met a new person and as they're talking about their past relationships, they just go off on an angry rant about their ex? It definitely quenches any spark anyone may have for you if you're still venting about a past relationship. Dwelling in resentment is an anvil around your neck that drags you down, and it effectively fends off any hope of a new positive relationship in your future.

And finally, though some would swear this is not so, please know that healing is never aided through vengeance. Vengeance begets more vengeance. If you get caught at your dastardly deed, you will have created a cycle of vengeance that can continue between you and the abuser way into the future. If you "get away with it" you are still tied to that person, and whether you feel remorse or not, you've sealed yourself to them through your vengeance. You will be more likely to continue to rent that free space as you either dwell on the satisfaction you have from your mean act, you plan more meanness to add to what you've done, or you regret and feel badly for what you did.

The other option? _Forgiveness_. The challenging truth is that healing and moving on with your life involves forgiveness. How do you understand forgiveness in a way that doesn't make you feel weak, duped or victimized? Some basic truths; Forgiveness is an *internal* process and may never even be shared with the person you're forgiving. Forgiveness doesn't mean restoring the relationship. Boundaries and even no contact may be entirely warranted and has nothing to do with forgiving.

Forgiving means to accept the reality of what happened, to grieve, to integrate the experience, to release it and the person, and to move on.

Accepting the event doesn't mean it was ok; what happened was likely awful, horrible, and even despicable. AND it happened. You didn't choose it and you can't reverse it. Nothing you can do will change this reality. Your only choices are in how you handle it now.

Grief, as we've discussed, is essential. Grieve over your loss of the relationship with the one who hurt you, or your imaginings of what the relationship would turn out to be, or whatever other losses this loss caused. It's critical to spend time allowing your sadness to be felt, expressed, cried out, journaled about, whatever it takes. Grief always involves many aspects including anger, what if's, sadness, denial, and you can wander in and out of these aspects many times. Take the time to come all the way around to acceptance and integration.

Integration is about internalizing the fact that you survived, you are strong, and that you can and will move forward in your life. Sometimes during this time you ponder what you could have done to protect yourself better, or what you will do differently in the future. This is not about self-blame, and you need to be careful not to get down on yourself, but at times you do learn to have stronger boundaries or make other commitments to yourself in the future. This may involve anything from blocking all contact with a person, to filing for a protective order, or police reports, or it may involve being more emotionally distant to someone who is hurtful to you.

Letting Go; Breathe, pray, meditate, or visualize letting go of the person, your resentment, and all of the emotional baggage you have carried. If you need help, there are many relaxation/visualization apps available. Be aware of this letting go, and realize it is a process, not a one-time event. You may need to work on this for weeks or months, so as you practice, notice the release, even if it comes only in tiny baby steps. Internalize the messages; it happened, it's in the past; I'm not going to give it my future; I'm going to release this now; I'm done with it; I don't have to let it live on in my body and mind; I'm releasing the anger and resentment. Over time you may find a lightening of your mood, less anxiety, and less depression. You may find the toxic person seems smaller and incapable of being powerful over you ever again. Work to inhale a sense of calm strength to take the place of anger and bitterness. As you reclaim your internal space, notice it, and savor it.

You may be thinking, 'yeah, but you don't know what they did to me, I can't forgive that.' Remember, this is for *you*, not *them*; this is a release of the anger and resentment you don't want to carry for the rest of your life. You will carry it until you stop carrying it, it will make you sick, and can even kill you, it will keep you from being close to anyone again and will keep you seething in bitterness. What happened, happened; your choices are to become bitter or to become better. Do you want to release it or carry it? Choose to let go and move on with your life!

Journal; Write about your thoughts on anger, vengeance, resentment, and forgiveness. What are you realizing is still anchoring you down, poisoning you, or keeping you stuck?

Awareness of Ruminating;
Many people struggle mightily to stop ruminating about the abuser. They find they are literally obsessing over what the person is doing, thinking, feeling, wanting, or needing, and this takes over any healing that could be happening.
Let's remember why and how this rumination began. When in a relationship with a toxic person, your emotions, thoughts, and realities don't matter; only theirs matter. So as you spent time with them, they denied your reality, didn't care about your emotions, didn't acknowledge or validate your thoughts. Over time you forget about, invalidated, and denied your own thoughts, feelings, and realities. Your life, time, energy, and effort revolved around noticing their every mood, placating their every need, taking care of their every emotion. This does not stop when you leave; it can even intensify. Notice your ruminations on them as if they are a drug you are craving. In the same way, meth is not good for you, but if you're an addict, you will obsess on using again, rumination is you obsessing on this unhealthy person. Just as in detoxing from a drug, you need to remind yourself of

the negative consequences associated with this person and put healthier strategies and activities into your life to take the place of this rumination. You need to continually re-focus your thoughts onto yourself; your needs, dreams, thoughts, and emotions. It takes practice but is essential. Notice, re-focus, self-coach, and practice.

When you can hear your own self, validate your own emotions, thoughts, beliefs, and realities, and take care of yourself in all the above ways with care and compassion, then you will know you are healing. When you notice rumination begins to escalate again, see it as a drug-craving, and re-focus on you again.

Journal; When do you notice you tend to ruminate? What are the typical narratives you're ruminating on? What can you put into your thoughts instead? What activities would help you let go of ruminating and feel better in the moment?

CHAPTER 11; R IS FOR REBUILDING

<u>Rebuilding your sense of self;</u> The relationship with a toxic person is all about tearing you down so they can control and manipulate you. The longer you're in this relationship, the more broken you become. At this point it is imperative to take stock of how you feel about yourself, which, in the aftermath of an abusive relationship, likely isn't very good. In my experience, wonderful people often feel completely unlovable in these early stages. It's essential to realize that this experience has nothing to do with who you are, and how lovable you are. They tore you down to control you, they said the things that hurt to destroy your sense of self, and to undermine your strengths. Their words were never true, just very pointed, and painful. They were surgical in their strikes; they zeroed in on the most tender spots in your heart during their attacks and left you in an emotional wasteland. But none of it was based in any fact; it was simply the thing they knew would bring you to your knees, and make you feel undone, so they could re-conform you to their liking. Rebuilding your inner sense of self is a huge part of what the journey back is all about. More than likely you're a kind, caring, empathic, and giving person; all really good qualities, but also qualities that set you up for hurt when shared with an abusive person. Reclaiming those wonderful qualities and promising yourself you will only share them with other empathic people, lays the crucial foundation for your new sense of self.

<u>Understanding self-esteem</u>; Back in the 1980's there was a "self-esteem movement" that honestly was a real train-wreck. If you were raised during that time or affected by it, you may have a lot of confusion over why you have low self-esteem, and how to improve it. Let's outline the myths and truths, and help you find a

healthier sense of self.

The Myths:

1. Saying over and over in the mirror, "I like myself," will improve my self-esteem. Nope, trying to brainwash yourself from self-hatred into self-love doesn't work. While you're standing there you're usually arguing inside your head, then trying harder to drown out that ugly voice, then arguing harder, then getting discouraged that you "can't even do that right," and hating yourself more. You are smarter than this; you can't brainwash yourself; you have to be able to combat your self-hatred with something real and solid, not empty "I like myself."

2. If everyone gets a participation ribbon, self-esteem will go up. Not even close. This was part of the self-esteem movement, and it was a giant flop. It didn't improve self-esteem at all and watered down children's experiences in the process. It hampered their ability to strive, to compete, to experience frustration, to learn, grow, and become resilient. Kids need to experience doing hard things, putting in great effort, and getting results. They need to be part of teams working together well, to learn how great that feels, and what happens when teams don't work well together at all. They need to experience getting disappointed, stepping back, looking at what went wrong, adjusting, and trying harder.

3. Telling kids they are awesome, wonderful, and beautiful all the time will help their self-esteem. Nope. It makes them arrogant, distant from others, and gives them no real information about their unique and vital character qualities. They learn nothing about who they are and what their lives are about. This is probably the most damaging myth as it confused kids and made them feel anxious and empty inside. Kids need to understand themselves in the context of their true strengths, and challenges; to see themselves within the context of their

family, the community, their school and other social situations. They need to feel a sense of participation, and a sense of mattering. This includes struggling through homework, playing on a sports team, doing chores to help out, learning to share with a sibling, friend, or teammate, and working through hard times with determination, and diligence. They need to know they are not always the center of attention, they need to learn to be humble, polite, empathic, and to own up for their mistakes. Just telling them they are the best, the brightest, and the most handsome or beautiful, focuses them on their superficial external attributes, and sets them up to be obsessed with the superficial, and either arrogant or empty, depending on how they look that day.

The Truth; The singular and most important truth is that our sense of self needs to be based on character qualities and values. These include our empathy, honesty, integrity, work ethic, effort, and relationships with others; including listening, responding with care, being intentional, leading with compassion vs bullying, assertiveness, boundaries, communications, and even being part of a team with awareness of others, and focus, versus selfishness and rebellion. The rest of the story is how we assess and then work on continuous improvement of these character qualities.

Meaning and Purpose; When you are living within your values, you gain a sense of meaning and purpose, which also enhances your sense of self. You don't have to change the world, but you can change *your* little part of it. Whether you bag groceries, or run a multinational corporation, how you show up determines how you feel about yourself and how others respond to you. Do you light up someone's day or ruin it? Does your presence in a room create warmth and collaboration, or conflict and frustration? Do you spread vicious rumors and get people at odds with each other, or bring people together and create a fun, creative, and enriching atmosphere? Are you living your values at work, home, or school? Take note of your strengths, and your challenges, and commit to living closer to your values each day.

<u>Celebrating, and improving:</u> When you see where you are living close to your values, and you like and respect your character qualities, take a moment to celebrate the miracle of who you are. Especially if you came from a childhood fraught with abuse or neglect, and yet, you're a loving, giving, empathic person, celebrate the miracle of enduring, surviving, and being yourself even in the midst of the trauma or challenges you endured. If there are areas you're not feeling good about, then focus time and attention on improving those. Pay attention to these attributes and improve your sense of living within your values and improving your character qualities. As you do, you will gain a more positive sense of self and feel continuously better about who you are.

<u>Self-esteem shines as a light from the inside out:</u> Often people think they are working to *become someone else*, but self-esteem is not an outfit you put on. Rather it is about *becoming your full, authentic self*, recognizing your strengths, your values, and living closer to those each day. When you've done this internal house-cleaning and stock-taking, your personality will shine through. You will know and feel the truths of who you are and have a new sense of respect for yourself.

<u>A Sense of Solidness:</u> Knowing these truths about yourself gives you a sense of centeredness and solidness. You're not rocked off your axis by others' antics. When you have a solid sense of self, others can be arrogant, rude, or unreasonable, and you don't take it on as yours. When others are directly or indirectly insulting, you recognize it's about them. Eleanor Roosevelt famously said, "No one can insult you if you don't participate". Think about that; if someone is insulting, and you have a solid sense of yourself, you just say inside your head, 'Wow, they must really have a disturbed sense of *themselves* to need to put me down in order to feel better. I wouldn't want to live in their skin.' And you move on. When your sense of self is strong and you feel centered, others' stuff is just that; *their* stuff. If you need to set boundaries, tell them something difficult that you know they don't want to hear, you

can do it without second-guessing yourself into paralysis.

Real Self-Esteem is Humble, Human, and Genuine; When this solid sense of self comes from inside, you don't have to brag, or attention-seek; you can take ownership of your faults and foibles, and you exude confidence from the inside out. When you're settled in your values and character qualities, you don't need superficial things in your life. You easily see others who are superficial for what they are; empty and like frosting on a turd; it might look nice but it's still a turd!

To know, respect, and love yourself is a very *simple* process, but not *easy*. It can take you back to some painful parts of childhood, and back through some of the abuse you endured from others since then. The hardest part is to look at the journey differently; focusing on your character qualities, your values, your sense of meaning, purpose, depth, and connectedness.

Journal; Take a few moments and write about your character qualities; are you kind, caring, empathic, honest, honorable, noble, able to be selfless when appropriate, strong, resilient, a caring mom or dad, brother or sister, daughter, son, or friend? What are your values and how well are you living them? If you're not sure, ask someone close to you to help you. Often, we don't see the positives in ourselves as easily as we see the negatives. Frequently those with the lowest self-esteem have great character qualities but they don't see them until asked to do this exercise. Recognizing these qualities, you can start to see that you actually like and respect who you are. Write about your strengths, (where you're living your values,) and your weak spots, (areas where you would like to live closer to your values,)

In what ways can you celebrate your strengths, and in what areas do you want to grow?

This journal information gives you some genuine truths about yourself that you can use to thwart the negative self-statements that might still pop up for you as you rebuild. Having solid self-statements like, "I'm very loyal, and trusting; good qualities

I respect about myself, but I need to set boundaries with people who are not trustworthy." When old self-hateful thoughts come up, you can combat them with your new truths. This is not brainwashing, or saying 'I like myself,' but telling yourself the *truth* about you. Keeping those positives in mind, you can clarify the self-improvements you want to make; 'I'm realizing I value listening but I'm not that good a listener; I'll make an effort to quiet my mind and listen better.' 'I'm not always completely honest and feel crummy when I don't tell someone my whole truth in the moment; I'm going to work on always being honest, whether it's comfortable or not.' 'I want to be the same person in every setting, so I feel like my integrity is solid. I'm going to pay attention to being myself, not being a chameleon, or people-pleaser.'

This is an ongoing growth journey and not a one-day event. We are continually growing into our sense of self, our sense of meaning and purpose, and our self-development. Don't think of this as something you do once but something you are aware of throughout every day. If you're feeling badly about yourself one day, ask yourself what's going on? Don't be afraid to spend a day to yourself, going back over your self-assessment and just being quiet. Notice if you're internally reacting to someone else's judgment or if you're disappointed that you're not living your values. If it's about someone else, recenter yourself on your truths. If you've disappointed yourself, spend time regrouping to live closer to who you know yourself to be.

<u>Becoming your own best friend;</u> Since the toxic person taught you to self-berate, self-hate, self-condemn and self-abuse. You will now have to work to begin to self-care and grow your self-compassion. You need to become your own best friend inside your head, instead of your own worst enemy. Continually notice your self-talk and do not allow yourself to perpetuate the abuse. Be as gentle and kind as you would if your best friend were going through this, and consciously become your own best friend.

Now that we've explored a lot about self-esteem, and how this builds an inner sense of trusting yourself, and feeling centered and grounded in yourself, notice how you know, respect, and appreciate who you are; your character qualities, strengths, and challenges.

Journal; What have you learned about you? Pull together all of your new insights into some solid statements that you can use to support and encourage yourself in this next chapter of your life.

Exploring what you feel, want, need, or think; When rebuilding after an abusive relationship, many people don't know even the basics of what they feel, need, want, or think. You've literally spent all of your energy, focus, and attention on someone else's wants, needs, feelings, dreams, passions, and thoughts. Spending time paying attention to yourself will be a challenge and one of the most important tasks ahead.

Journal; Notice and write about your needs, wants, emotions, thoughts, passions, and dreams. You may find this frustrating and hard but keep at it. When you find lost parts of yourself, old dreams, passions, wants, emotions, needs, pay attention and honor them. Ask yourself if there is a way to find new purpose and meaning in those old dreams, and passions. Sometimes this leads to a whole new direction, and some amazing things can come of these insights.

Rebuilding your connectedness; Another crucial part of the rebuilding journey involves recognizing and reversing the isolation the abuser created in your life. Isolating you kept you away from family and friends who could support you, make you feel good about yourself, or bring fun, joy, and enrichment to your life. It helped them gaslight you freely, knowing you had no one to help you make sense of it all. It was a crucial part of how they controlled you. Many people say they're too embarrassed to talk to friends and family, and they stay isolated, only to become easy prey for the abuser again. The truth is the people who *really* care about you will be happy to welcome you back into their lives, and will understand what happened if you share with them. If they're not welcoming, then you need to build new relationships with others.

Since the abuser took up all of your time and energy, you may be drawn back into the abusive relationship because you feel lonely and bored. Realize this may happen, and intentionally fill in the holes left in their wake with other people and activities. There are thousands of things to do and this is a great time to branch out, try something new, or even a little off the wall. Try something active if you can, or, if you're not as able to be active, look at volunteer opportunities in your area. There are many nonprofits needing help, and it can feel really good to be part of something bigger than what you're going through. It's a great way to get out of a rut, get out of your funk, and to connect with other empathic people. Regaining your sense of meaning and purpose, plus being around other people who are caring for others unselfishly, is really healthy.

<u>Loneliness;</u> Loneliness had become an 'epidemic' even prior to the COVID pandemic. Since then, it is clear that people's disconnectedness has gone from bad to worse. Loneliness is not about being alone; we can feel lonely in a crowd of family, friends, or colleagues. Loneliness is about feeling disconnected from others. Studies have shown that loneliness is linked to cardiovascular problems, poor sleep, and depleted immune function. In addition, loneliness lowers creativity and reasoning abilities, causes declines in workplace productivity, job satisfaction, and higher unemployment. In terms of mental health concerns, loneliness leads to higher rates of anxiety, depression, suicidality, as well as higher compulsive use of technology, drug, alcohol, and cigarette use, and self-harm.

In surveys to determine the factors that contribute to human happiness the most, respondents consistently rate 'connection to friends and family,' above wealth or fame, and even above physical health. Interestingly, laboratory research has examined the power of our need for contact with others and has mapped its physiological roots. Cooperation, empathy, and positive social interactions activate the "reward" areas of the brain, much as those areas are activated by the satisfaction of hunger. At the same time, social rejection activates the areas that light up when we are subjected to physical pain. These are powerful internal processes at work, so honor your need for connectedness through your actions as you rebuild.

Journal; How can you find some connectedness that will nurture you? What are the ways your relationship kept you alone, and what can you do now to push past this isolation? Write about a time you felt fearful of a new experience but did it anyway, and felt excited about the result?

Brainstorm some things you'd like to do. Choose a couple of them and look them up, making a plan for when you will pursue each one.

Notice the ways your life has become out of balance? In what areas could you rebuild new passions, hobbies, activities, or volunteer activities to enrich your life?

Write about specifics like; 'I've always wanted to be more adventurous; I'm going to join a hiking club, or get a bike, or go camping.' Or 'I've always wanted to feel more of a sense of meaning in my life; I'm going to look up volunteer opportunities in my area and pick something and go do it. If I don't like it, I'm not going to give up; I'll pick something else and try that.' Or 'I'm tired of going to bars and clubs, or online to meet people; it's so shallow; I'm going to give dating a rest and just rebuild myself and my life for a while.' Or 'I'm sick of wasting my time isolated playing video games/watching TV, I'm going to turn it off, get out and do things. I'll keep trying different things until I find some that really spark my sense of who I am and what my life is about.'

Self-Care;
When someone says you need to do more *self-care* do you draw a blank? Have you basically taken care of everyone else for so

long, you don't even know how to take care of yourself? You're in good company; there are many who struggle with self-care, so this section is for you. Each of us is unique, so some things will click for you and other things won't; know that it will take time to find what works for you.

First, let's take a moment to assess your current emotional and physical state.

<u>Journal</u>;
Are you emotionally drained? Do you feel completely tapped out, like if someone asks one more thing of you, you're likely to bite their head off, or completely implode and fall apart? Do you feel you've been doing so much for others for so long, you've lost yourself, lost your way, and fallen into despair? When you do have time to yourself, do you fall into a vegetative state in front of the TV, video games, or your phone?
Are you physically drained? Have you been on the go for so long, you feel like caffeine and other drugs are the only things holding your head up? Do you have to then take something to get to sleep because you're so jacked up, you can't wind down? Is the pure physical depletion and exhaustion from this cycle so debilitating that you've developed headaches and other ailments?
Or are you emotionally AND physically exhausted?

When you've been in an abusive relationship, whether for months, or even years, the stress of daily life causes rushes of adrenaline that, over time, cause a buildup of cortisol in your brain. This results in feeling exhausted but unable to sleep, as well as agitated, irritable, anxious, and depressed. For some, a visit to your doctor or finding a good psychiatrist may be necessary to help you rebalance your brain chemistry. But for most, healthy lifestyle changes will help you feel better. The basics of healthy sleep habits, healthy eating, and learning about self-calming techniques, will be enough to get you back to feeling good.

Let's start with some basics of physical self-care; The first and *most* important thing we can do is learn to *breathe.* Breathing deeply makes you an active part of your world, and not breathing well, is some sort of self-defeating attempt to *not* be part of life. Many people, in their extreme stress and self-neglect, don't know how to fully and deeply breathe. As I've worked with thousands of people over the years, I know this is more common than not. So, the first part of your self-care is to notice your breathing. Take time to just sit quietly. If you can find a space that is very peaceful, where the only sounds are natural sounds, that would be ideal, but anyplace can work. Breathe in and out deeply and slowly. Imagine that your lungs are balloons, and you are inflating them all the way into your diaphragm on every in-breath, and collapsing them completely on every out-breath. Sit and do this for several minutes, gradually slowing and deepening your breathing. Notice how everything calms and slows within you.

The second most basic and crucial thing is how we nourish ourselves. We need at least a gallon of water, and many colors of fruits and vegetables to nourish these bodies every day. In the devastation of the abusive relationship, have you resorted to self-soothing through unhealthy food? It may seem obvious, and many of you will glaze over and turn the page, but let's be honest; ingesting dead, processed food all day every day is truly poisoning you. And since you are trying to get rid of toxic people in your lives, you must also take a look at other toxic habits. You may not be able to do this all at once, but just for today, let go of something unhealthy and add in something nourishing. Watch some documentaries about what healthy and unhealthy food does to your emotions as well as your physical body, and work to incorporate more plants, and let go of processed foods.

Sleep; Your physical depletion may be due to some unhealthy sleep habits. In the past you may not have been able to choose how and when to sleep. Some abusers specifically control through sleep deprivation, interruption, and other means of exhausting and depleting you. In your rebuilding, you will need to take back your rest by intentionally choosing a healthy bedtime, winding down with a good book, shutting off all technology 2 hours ahead of that time, and getting as close as you can to 8 hours of sleep. This may seem daunting at first, but it is another very crucial aspect of your self-care and will yield incredible benefits if you find and stick to healthy sleep habits.

Moving your body; this goes along with breathing and nourishing. Our bodies were created to move, and when we move, we feel better. Conversely, our sedentary lives keep us sick. Again, you can't shift it all overnight, but do something, anything from simple stretching, to walking, running, hiking, water activities like swimming, water-walking in a pool, kayaking, paddle boarding, the list is endless. Pick something, try it out, and find what will work for you and your body. There are even chair yoga, tai chi and other stretches for anyone who is not able to do more active things.

Rejuvenating Rest; We often get confused about whether to rest or not, and how to rest. If you're not getting enough sleep, or if your life is physically demanding as well as mentally fatiguing, you may need to rest. But most of us are emotionally exhausted, not physically tired. Furthermore, if you are physically tired, most people don't recognize that plugging into TV and other screens to 'rest,' does not rejuvenate you, but only fatigues your mind as well. Studies are clear on this; screens are mentally fatiguing. They do shift your attention off of your stressful thought processes, so we think of them as restful, but they really just distract for a time and don't accomplish anything else. If you are physically fatigued, you need more sleep, but if you are emotionally exhausted, you need to get out and move. At the end of a workday, I'm exhausted, but the weariness is mental/emotional, not physical. Even though I don't always feel like it, I know I need to walk, ride my bike, get on my rowing machine, and I find every time, that movement rejuvenates me. Resting when emotionally drained can even be *counterproductive* and actually make you feel worse.

Self-care guilt; Notice the internal messages in your mind around self-care. Many people notice they feel guilty when they take care of themselves, and this keeps them from following through. It's important to remember this self-critical voice is part of your old story. Let your new self-compassion steer your ship. Empower the voice that is genuinely you. Be gentle with yourself. Act as if you are taking your best friend out for a day of rejuvenation. Talk to yourself kindly, encouragingly, supportively. Ask yourself what would feel good, what would positively impact you right now, what would be healthy and rejuvenating?

Slow down and notice how this feels. Begin to notice how it feels to just be present with yourself. This may be fleeting as your thoughts will still bounce around, but with practice, you will get better at staying in the moment. Be still, quiet your thoughts, notice nature, notice how your body and mind feel quieter. And savor this. As you savor, internalize this feeling, memorize it so you can take it with you into the busier part of your life. Learning to quiet and calm yourself, staying present, supporting, and nurturing yourself will become a state you can bring with you wherever you go.

Make a commitment to practice this calming and quieting daily. One of the myths that keeps us stuck on the burn-out roller coaster is feeling there is nothing short of quitting your job and running away that will make any positive impact. But this isn't true; we can all make a *daily* practice of self-calming, self-nurturing, self-nourishing, and being part of nature. We can learn to distinguish between physical and mental/emotional fatigue and take effective action to find more balance. Check into an app like Calm, or Breathe, or Insight Timer, and spend some time learning self-calming techniques; these will bring down the cortisol levels in your brain over time and can be key in feeling better.

Spiritual; For some people, self-care is rooted in their spiritual beliefs. Finding or reconnecting with God, Higher Power or whatever you find as your source of spiritual well-being, can be crucial in grounding your sense of healing, balance, purpose, and meaning.

<u>Clear out toxic substances.</u> Have you become reliant on any substances for self-soothing or escape? What substances can you let go of to improve your health and balance?

<u>Restorative Time</u>; What is JOMO? It's the opposite of FOMO and stands for; The Joy Of Missing Out! Yes, it's not only a thing, it's a *good* thing! By letting go of the frenetic, anxiety producing busyness, you can actually improve your creativity, your health, and your emotional wellness.

Missing out means to spend time on your own, relaxing, breathing in nature, being in the moment, finding time for self-care, and turning off your media. It's to find or re-find the joy of peace, serenity, and downtime. The constant attention-demanding tasks, the non-stop barrage of digital media, the noise of urban environs, and other sources of constant bombardment are causing Cognitive Fatigue. It wears us out, makes us sick, and causes or exacerbates a lot of our anxiety and depression. When our downtime is still filled with TV, video games, checking our phones, there is no rest for our weary minds.

Restorative time happens when we intentionally reduce the demands on our executive-based attention, allowing ourselves the soft-focus of relaxing in a natural environment. There are thousands of ways to engage in restorative time for yourself, and we each need to find what works for us.

In 2009 Japanese scientists studied "forest bathing" (taking time in nature), and recognized *dramatic decreases in stress hormones,* including cortisol. Cortisol results from trauma, and other chronic stress, and its presence in the brain leads to irritability, sleep problems, anxiety, and depressive symptoms. If spending time in nature decreases cortisol, this is a significant finding indeed!

The study also found an *increase in the white blood cell count* which means forest bathing *strengthens our immune systems.*

Other studies in 2012 and 2014 *validated decreased stress hormones, and decreases in anxiety and depressive symptoms.*
Another study in 2019 concluded that we need more time being *bored if we want to recoup our creativity*! In our culture, we spend a lot of time and energy avoiding boredom, while it turns out, we actually *need* to allow ourselves some quiet, non-structured time, some boredom, in order to allow this restorative time to stimulate our creativity.

Retreat; If you can, go on a retreat for a weekend, or a week, do it! But even if you can only muster small retreats for a day or part of a day, anything will be helpful. Take an inspiring book, a great cup of tea or coffee, curl up in a quiet spot to just be with you. Learn to be at peace within yourself and with yourself. Even if it's a walk or sitting for a time outside, it's crucial to make nature part of your self-care. For me I need to spend time in places where there are only natural sounds; places where I can see trees and water, or wide-open spaces. If you live in a city and this isn't possible, find a park, or your yard, or even create a peaceful spot in your home with some plants and other things you find soothing to feed this need. If you are stuck inside, shut off all of the technology, allow quiet time, gently notice your thoughts, and let each go, put on soothing music, or listen to ocean or rain sounds. (There are apps you can download with ocean or rain sounds.)

Taking a break gives us the peace we need to embrace a calmer, quieter internal state, which helps us create relationships that are more balanced, nurturing and reciprocal. When we become internally quiet, internally self-appreciative, and self-knowing, we will not connect with someone who pulls us back into drama; we just won't let that happen. Our self-awareness being internally calm and strong, gives us a keener awareness of what others are really made of. Our creep-o-meter will go off when we run into another toxic person, and we will not wander into that minefield again.

So for our creativity, physical health, as well as our emotional wellness, we need restorative time, ideally in nature, and ideally without any cognitive demands.

Journal: Are you physically, or emotionally exhausted, or both? What do you typically do to rejuvenate? Is it working? What would you say would probably be healthier? What can you commit to doing differently this week? What would be some longer-term goals? How can you pay closer attention to how you rejuvenate throughout your day, after work, and on your days off? What would you want to plan for a truly rejuvenating vacation in the future?

What ways have you started to nurture your emotions, and what do you want to commit to doing each day to honor and nurture yourself emotionally?

What healthy living changes have you made and what are you wanting to change to help yourself improve your physical health? Be specific regarding sleep, eating, activity and self-calming strategies.

Where are you in your spiritual healing? What activities can you incorporate to help you find or enhance your conscious contact with God or your sense of a Higher Power or even a healthier self?

In what ways has your occupational or educational life suffered in this relationship? Do you want to reclaim your passions or dreams to get back to school, or a job, or career you de-railed, or find something new?

How are you doing socially? Do you want to find new social connections? Can you join a new group/club/meet up/church/volunteer opportunity to improve your social connectedness?

What are some ways you already enjoy time in nature? What are some ideas you can implement today? Next week? Next month?
Self-care strategies are crucial when you're coming out of an abusive relationship and are trying to regroup and recoup yourself and your life. No one will do this for you, and mental, emotional, and physical fatigue over time, can literally kill you. Be good to

you! You're the only one who can begin to know what is going on within you and decide what you need to do to take better care of you, so learn what works for you, and commit to it.

Conquering Codependence;
Codependence is the over dependence on others for your sense of self, sense of safety, and sense of mattering. If you feel empty, scared, and worthless whenever you're alone; if you only feel complete, content and happy when others are filling you up; if it takes others to make you feel confident, competent, safe, or worthwhile, you're codependent. In a sense, codependency is the compulsive need for a person/or people, much the same way alcohol dependence is a compulsive need for alcohol. When we are codependent, we keep ourselves in unhealthy relationships with toxic people, including partners, irresponsible or drug addicted adult children, draining friends, or toxic family members. Codependents don't set sensible boundaries, or end relationships when they need to. They tend to enable and rescue instead of letting go. They can be so enabling and rescuing that their loved one can't possibly grow up or become mature or independent. Codependency exists in a range from mild to severe, and can be as serious as alcohol, drug, or any other dependency.

Journal; As you read the above description, who (in addition to the abusive relationship) can you identify as a focus of your codependency. What do you have to have from them to feel ok? Do you have to talk to them every day? See them every day? How do you feel when you don't? What is your behavior like when you don't get from them what you feel you want or need? What do you put up with from them that you know you shouldn't put up with? What do you not say, or even lie about because of your codependency on them? In what ways have you enabled and rescued and how is this affecting their growing up?
What boundaries do you know you need to set and yet you feel too afraid because you might lose them?
How much is your behavior based on fear of being abandoned by

them?

If you find yourself alone a lot; here is a separate set of questions; Do you ever feel people are distancing from you, or pushing away because you came on too strong, were too clingy, needed too much from them, were smothering or suffocating them? Often, we find we get into a cycle of demanding attention from others, and then feeling guilty for needing so much from them. This is ultimately unsatisfying and not at all the same as when two whole people share time together.

A codependent relationship has no space for either person to have their own friends, interests, or time apart. The insecurity is too intense. When you *need* a person versus wanting to spend time together, you will manipulate and pressure when you don't get the attention you need. It's like the difference between *needing* to drink and just having a casual drink. When you are addicted, you feel a compulsion to drink; your time, attention, focus, energy, and intensity are on that drink, and if anyone stands in your way, they will get mowed down. Codependency carries that intensity of compulsivity with it. You have to have that attention, that support, that bolstering ,or you feel empty and lost. Taking this inventory will help you begin to notice this dynamic. As you pay attention, you will notice how this happens throughout every day, and then you will begin to know how it's affecting your relationship with yourself, and others.

Recovery from codependency means becoming a whole person, and your own best friend. You have to push past the discomfort of spending time alone, learn about yourself, embrace who you are, and what your life is about; the good, the bad, and the ugly. We've journaled about this a lot in the section on Self-Care,

Recognize that you are a unique individual, and others are also completely unique. As this really settles in, you can fully realize that tying your worth to someone else's fleeting thoughts, feelings, or attitudes about you is absurd. Leo Buscalia used to say, "If you're a grape aspiring to be a melon, you're always going to feel like a failure; you'll always see yourself as too small, too insignificant, too purple." This sounds like a silly analogy but it's so true; you can only work to be the best *you*. You cannot compare yourself to anyone else and feel good about yourself. Your journey, attributes, and character are uniquely you, and these all combine to give you the abilities, and gifts to share with others that are uniquely yours. When you realize this, you begin to see how your gifts can create the life you feel good about. Be the best you; develop your best qualities, work to love your worth.

Learn to fill yourself up. The myth underlying codependency is that you are empty, and others are there to fill you, complete you, and make you feel better. This is just not true. It's no one else's job to fill you or complete you, and the sooner you really get this, the happier you will be. When you lean on others for what is your responsibility, you will get a lot of pushing away, resentment, and drama in your relationships. When you start to fill yourself, you will find you are a complete and whole person, who can offer a richness to others. Finding that sense of internal quiet, self-calming, setting time aside daily to breathe, meditate or pray, will help you recharge, rejuvenate, and refill yourself from your source. When you are able to do this consistently, you can feel whole, without asking someone else to fill you or make you whole. As a whole person, capable of recharging yourself, you can begin to think of togetherness as two wholes sharing and caring about each other. Your relationships can then become healthy, reciprocal, relaxed, and enjoyable. Neither is over-dependent on the other, both are complete and enjoy their alone time and their together time. You can give each other space and enjoy seeing each other with new thoughts and experiences to share. When you have something difficult to say or a boundary to set, speak it; only those who disrespect and disregard you will not accept truth and boundaries, and you don't want them in your life anyway. As you speak truth and boundaries, you will naturally weed out those who use and abuse you, and you will be free of their abuse and drama.

Broaden your world; typically, codependent people shrink their world in order to feel more in control, less afraid, and more able to manage fewer things and people. But when you are a whole, solid self, you can expand your world to include many different people, activities, volunteer interests, and adventures. As you expand your world, notice how this builds your sense of self. Since we do get some of our best understanding of who we are through feedback from others, this expansion of our world can be very enriching. Strike out on an adventure on your own, without solid plans and with some risk. This is the best way to see how you handle life's hurdles and challenges, and to develop a stronger sense of self and wholeness.

In summary, become your own best friend, take care of yourself, learn to fill yourself from your source, speak your truth and set boundaries, broaden your world, and then greet others from a whole person perspective. This is what is meant by *interdependence*. It's a much better, happier, more contented, state than codependence, and will lead to happier, more connected and secure relationships

Journal;
Write about what you need to do to feel more whole. Write how your relationships would be different if you came to them from a whole person perspective. How would you speak your truth, stand up to others, stop rescuing, placating, and enabling if you didn't fear being abandoned?

CHAPTER 12; STRESS STRATEGIES

Stress is something we all deal with, to some degree, all the time. When healing from toxic relationships, we will be handling more than ever. In addition, your stress system has already been overloaded for many months or years. The physical and emotional effects of stress tear you down in serious ways. While you can't rid your life of stress, you can take care of your stress differently and this will radically change how you feel and how you are able to cope.

Some of what troubles us is the demand itself, and the rest of the stress is how we *react* to the demand. For example, the work you have to complete is a clear real demand on your time and attention which is causing a certain amount of stress. But the way you talk to yourself internally either calms you or escalates you. If your internal chatter is; 'I can't do this, this is too much, too hard, I hate this, I'm such an idiot, I hate this job/class/house, and I just want to quit,' you're going to be miserable, AND stressed. If instead, your internal chatter is, 'You got this, just do this part now and take a break, you can do this, it's challenging but it's going to be great when you accomplish it,' then your stress is just the job and not the add-on of your negative stories.

Recognize that the internal narrative is yours to choose. I had a professor in graduate school at the University of Connecticut who said many times during every lecture, "Pain is inevitable, misery, however, is optional." I could rewrite this to say, "Stress is inevitable; freaking out over it, however, is optional." We tend to add so much stress to our stress by how we internally torture ourselves. Your internal narrative can be encouraging or paralyzing. It's your choice every minute of every day. Notice what your usual narratives are, and how this impacts your stress.

<u>The myth of multitasking.</u> It's crucial to realize that you can do one thing at a time well, or many things at a time poorly. I

was a lifelong multi-tasker, (now in recovery,) but it turns out multitasking is a myth. Studies show we are actually doing a bunch of things poorly and causing ourselves a lot of stress by bouncing from thing to thing to thing. It takes on average, 11 minutes to get back on focus after a distraction, so we're actually giving some of our attention to each thing, continually losing focus, and mired in distraction after distraction. The truth is, if we do one thing at a time, complete it, or a section of it, and then intentionally move on to the next, we lessen our stress.

Learn to divide your list into *immediate, important, foundational, and visionary*. The immediate is on your list for today; the important you'll also get to if you can; the foundational is stuff you want to do to build on your future; and the visionary is stuff you dream about. When you divide your demands this way, you can get focused and stay on track for each day.

Begin the day with a plan; As a supervisor, I was constantly pressed to multitask, and react to everyone and everything coming at me from the time I arrived until I left for the day. A strategy I used to help lessen this craziness was to start every morning with my door closed, while I got organized and made a plan. When you are proactive, you feel more in control and less freaked out. Regroup at lunchtime and see what you've accomplished and what's still needing your attention.

<u>Self-awareness and self-care</u>; Think of your stress on a 1-10 scale, with 1 being totally calm, and 10 being completely overwhelmed. The more time you spend between 1 and 5, the more productive you are. When you are emotionally distraught, your thought processes are diminished, your ability to be focused or productive is diminished, and the less focused and productive you are, the more overwhelmed you become, so you are soon in a self-escalating spin out. Breathe, do one thing at a time, and do it with a 1 to 5 calmness level. If you get to 6, take a break, take a walk, and remind yourself that nothing good happens between 6 and 10. Nothing!

<u>Learn to create your best work/rest cycles.</u> Take ten-minute breaks every hour or two, depending on how you're doing. If

you're getting bogged down, take a break. Make sure your breaks are healthy and rejuvenating; go outside, breathe, stretch, chat with a friend in the break room. Don't get on your phone, check social media on your computer, etc. Give your mind a rest. Remember the science in the self-care section; when we rest our minds and allow space, we are more productive and creative. Nature, in particular, is vital to rejuvenating us, so if you can take a brisk walk outside or do some stretching, this will be helpful. After ten minutes, jump back into your work. You'll be amazed at how much more productive you feel when you practice these strategies.

<u>Learn to reframe the stresses that bug you the most</u>. For example, if you hate your commute, find some great podcasts or audible books to make your commute more fulfilling and less frustrating. When picking up after your kids for the umpteenth time, or doing a pile of dishes, or cleaning your apartment at the end of a grueling day, turn on music and dance around while you work. One of my favorite pieces of science is that listening to music has been shown to illuminate and re-energize the positive chemistry and activity in our brains. When we sing to music, our brains are even more lit up, and when we play an instrument and sing with others, it's a New-Year's-Eve-in-Times-Square kind of explosion! So, find ways to change the *attitude of drudgery* into a *spirit of fun and fulfillment*. When you reframe these types of stressors in a more positive light, you will feel less stressed by them.

Celebrate each success; be encouraging and not negative. This includes giving yourself an internal, 'Yay, you did it!' every time you accomplish something.

And finally, reinforce it all by wrapping up your day with a <u>self-assessment;</u> how did you do with managing your stressors today? Did you list your stressors; notice the internal 'freak out' voice and calm it down; did you organize your day; did you breathe; did you do one thing at a time; did you take healthy breaks; did you make the drudgery fun; and did you celebrate each success?

Handling stress differently is another part of changing the

relationship with yourself from one of self-degradation, to one of support, encouragement, and celebration.

Journal:
Make a list of all of your most troubling stressors; what is bugging you? What weighs on your mind constantly? What demands your attention? Put them in categories like work, school, home, family, friends, life, etc.

Write about the emotional stories you're telling yourself that actually escalates that stress. Write about how you have bought into the myth of multitasking, commit to making lists, and doing one thing at a time. What drudgery would you like to reframe? How can you give yourself more encouragement throughout every day?

CHAPTER 13; LOVING AGAIN... OR NOT?!

In deciding to love again or stay single, make sure you spend a lot of time healing before you even let yourself ponder getting involved with someone else. Sadly, many people don't take the time, and end up in a similar relationship and going through the cycles of abuse all over again. We relive the old relationship when we haven't healed from those old internal messages, haven't taken stock, or gone through this journey of exploration. So take the time it takes to really heal and rebuild so that you make a great choice next time. Most of all, learn to enjoy your time with YOU!

If you decide to get involved again, don't be in a rush. Don't get caught in the beliefs that you're getting old or there's no one out there for you or any of those old stories. Be patient; it truly is better to be alone than to be with another toxic person, and if you jump back in with the wrong person, you'll be missing out on the right one.

Be so present with yourself and so caring for yourself that when you meet someone who isn't, you know it and have no problem seeing them for what they are.

Practice standing up for yourself and walking away from toxic people. In small ways, and large, speak up, say your truth, and recognize it is not your job to rescue, placate, peace-keep, or help everyone else in the world to your detriment. Many empathic people think they are "not a good person" if they set boundaries or are not doing everything they can to "be there" for someone who "needs" them. Often the beginnings of a toxic relationship prey on this "be there" thing. Let me clarify; if you choose to help someone or be friends with someone who is needy and you want to help out, by all means do so, but know your limits, and never seek to be

in a *relationship* with someone like that. Which leads to the most important phrase I want to impress upon you;
Find a partner not a project! This means the person you're looking for is like you; empathic, kind, caring, loving, giving. If they are not any of these things, move on. If they are inconsistent in caring or giving or loving and are periodically really mean or vicious or selfish or hurtful, move on. If you are already on a roller coaster of hurt feelings and apologies, move on. Helping others is great, being there for someone who is challenging and needs loving support is wonderful, but your *partner* is your refuge from the world and from the hectic and painful aspects of life. If you don't feel a sense of peace in your partnership, and a sense of rejuvenation and revitalization from your time together, it won't get any better or easier when you add the challenges of life later. Don't settle; find that person who is fun, supportive, interesting, and gives you a sense of home.
Carefully review the sections, My empathy is killing me, and Developing a trustworthy creep-o-meter. Share honestly with your trusted family/friend/therapist, so that you're not letting things go that are red flags, and make sure you keep your wise mind onboard, and steering your ship.

M. Scott Peck said, "Love is caring about another's growth". Someone who loves you, loves to see you happy, wants to be closer, to grow closer, to see you live your best and healthiest life, to find and fulfill your highest goals and dreams. They are empathic and loving and they are *consistently* this way. When stress happens, they pull together with you, and work together on solutions; they don't become hateful and hostile, attacking and berating.

Deciding to stay single is a wonderful option! Make sure you allow and honor your desire to stay single. Let go of the societal judgements that may have driven you into unhealthy relationships in the past and let yourself find your completeness in all of the healing we've been talking about. Find companionship with like-minded friends, family, and find your sense of meaning, purpose, and closeness in how you choose to spend your time with caring empathic people.

Journal: What are your current thoughts and feelings about whether to love again or stay single? If you are deciding to love again, which awarenesses and strategies are most important as you move forward? If you're staying single, how can you support and celebrate your decision?

CHAPTER 14; HABITS VS. MOTIVATION

As you're going through this book and making changes in your life, I want to clarify something really important. Most people think of motivation as something you *have* or *don't have*. If you have it, that's great, and if you don't, then you're waiting for it to suddenly spring upon you. Until it does, you can't change anything in your life because you 'just don't have the motivation.' This is just not so! The science behind change is that we make a *decision* with our wise mind to change, we choose to change specific *habits*, and then we *do* those habits over and over, thus creating change. If you want your life to be different, you have to *decide* with your wise mind (not your emotional mind), then choose which *habits* need to change to make that happen, *commit* to doing those new habits and not the old. When you do this, you will see results, you will feel good about the results, and then you may get a *feeling* of motivation to continue to do those good habits. For some, the motivation feeling doesn't happen at all, and you just keep doing the good habits to get the good results you want, letting go of the myth that any of this comes from some magical motivation feeling that some have, and some don't.

Journal; What changes do you want to see in your life?
What habits do you need to change in order to see those changes? List bad habits you want to let go of, as well as good habits you'd like to adopt.
What are a few things you commit to change today?
What are a few short-term goals you can set for the next week, month, six months?

CHAPTER 15; FINAL THOUGHTS AND JOURNALING

Coming out of the FOG is about recognizing the Fear, Obligation and Guilt that blinded you into paralysis. As you explored how it all came about, you found the signals you ignored and the red flags you didn't perceive. Living in the CLEAR is about finding the radar-reality that gives you Clarity; Leaving the relationship, either emotionally or physically; Educating yourself about empathy, boundaries, and a strong, trustworthy creep-o-meter; growing your Awareness; and Rebuilding your sense of self and your life. I hope you have learned and grown throughout this journaling journey, and I want to encourage you to embrace your life passionately, continue to grow in your self-compassion, and in your new skills to support, encourage, and rejuvenate yourself every day.

Final journaling points;

What are your main take-aways or insights from this experience?
What changes have you noticed in yourself over the course of this journaling journey?
What further changes are you still working on?
How can these take-aways inform your short-term goals, medium term goals, long term goals?
Can you commit to journaling in an ongoing way, to keep accountability for these insights, changes, and goals?

You've emerged out of the FOG and into the CLEAR. Take good care of yourself, and we'll talk again soon!

Please let me know how you experienced this book/journal/workbook by emailing me at;

shannon.petrovich@TherapistTalks.com

ABOUT THE AUTHOR

Shannon D. Petrovich,

Shannon earned her bachelor's degree from Bowdoin College and her Master's in Social Work from the University of Connecticut School of Social Work. She completed her clinical licenses in Social Work and Substance Abuse Counseling in 1990, earned her Board Certified Diplomate in Clinical Social Work license in 2016, and has been a therapist for over 35 years.

She has worked in inpatient, outpatient, and residential settings, and is currently in private practice.

See also TherapistTalks.com website and TherapistTalks videos on YouTube.

Made in the USA
Monee, IL
02 June 2022